Senses of Devotion

art for faith's sake series

SERIES EDITORS:

Clayton J. Schmit
J. Frederick Davison

This series of publications is designed to promote the creation of resources for the church at worship. It promotes the creation of two types of material, what we are calling primary and secondary liturgical art.

Like primary liturgical theology, classically understood as the actual prayer and practice of people at worship, primary liturgical art is that which is produced to give voice to God's people in public prayer or private devotion and art that is created as the expression of prayerful people. Secondary art, like secondary theology, is written reflection on material that is created for the sake of the prayer, praise, and meditation of God's people.

The series presents both worship art and theological and pedagogical reflection on the arts of worship. The series title, *Art for Faith's Sake,* indicates that, while some art may be created for its own sake, a higher purpose exists for arts that are created for use in prayer and praise.

OTHER VOLUMES IN THIS SERIES:

Senses of the Soul by William A. Dyrness
Dust and Prayers by Charles L. Bartow
Dust and Ashes by James L. Crenshaw
Preaching Master Class by William H. Willimon
Praying the Hours in Ordinary Life by Clayton J. Schmit and Lauralee Farrer
Mending a Tattered Faith: Devotions with Dickinson by Susan VanZanten

FORTHCOMING VOLUMES IN THIS SERIES:

Blessed: Monologues for Mary by Jerusha Matsen Neal
Dance in Scripture: How Biblical Dancers Can Revolutionize Worship Today by Angela M. Yarber
Sanctifying Art: Inviting Conversation between Artists, Theologians, and the Church by Deborah Sokolove
ReVisioning: Critical Methods of Seeing Christianity in the History of Art edited by James Romaine and Linda Stratford

* *Art for Faith's Sake* is a phrase coined by art collector and church musician, Jerry Evenrud, to whom we are indebted.

Senses of Devotion

*Interfaith Aesthetics
in Buddhist and Muslim Communities*

William Dyrness

CASCADE *Books* · Eugene, Oregon

SENSES OF DEVOTION
Interfaith Aesthetics in Buddhist and Muslim Communities

Art for Faith's Sake 7

Cascade Books
An Imprint of Wipf and Stock Publishers
199 W. 8th Ave., Suite 3
Eugene, OR 97401

www.wipfandstock.com

ISBN 13: 978-1-62032-136-2

Cataloging-in-Publication data:

Dyrness, William A.

Senses of devotion : interfatih aesthetics in Buddhist and Muslim communities / William A. Dyrness.

xii + 148 p. ; 23 cm. — Includes bibliographical references.

Art for Faith's Sake 7

ISBN 13: 978-1-62032-136-2

1. Buddhist Art and Symbolism. 2. Islamic Art and Symbolism. 3. Aesthetics—Religious aspects. I. Title. II. Series.

BR115.A8 D97 2013

Manufactured in the U.S.A.

Table of Contents

Preface

This ethnographic study focuses on the religious practices and visual environment of five Buddhist temples and five Muslim mosques in Southern California. This study follows up an earlier study of Christian worship practices that I carried out with a group of student researchers from 2006–2008, funded by the Henry Luce Foundation. That study began as an attempt to understand the relationships between art and worship in the various Christian traditions. Early in our interviews, we discovered it was impossible to separate responses to images from reactions to other elements of worship, and the inquiry soon developed into a more holistic examination of the role of ritual practice, visual imagery, and even spatial arrangements in worship. That study was published in 2009.[1] With the encouragement of the Henry Luce Foundation we decided it would be appropriate to extend our research into other religious traditions, and we proposed to add Buddhist and Muslim communities to the study of Christian worship and to our parallel, smaller study of Jewish congregations.[2] To make comparison possible, we decided that we would, as far as possible, ask the same or similar questions to members of other communities that we had asked to the Christian congregants. The results of the some seventy-five hour-long interviews in the various Buddhist and Muslim communities are presented in this book.[3] The samples were chosen in accordance with what is called purposeful sampling. That is we sought "to understand certain select cases in their own right rather than to generalize to a population." In analyzing the results, it looks for "important shared patterns cutting across cases."[4]

1. See Dyrness, *Senses of the Soul: Art and the Visual in Christian Worship.*

2. The Jewish research in four congregations was conducted by PhD student Leah Buturain Schneider. That study has not yet been published.

3. See the appendix for the various protocols and interview sites.

4. Isaac and Michael, *Handbook in Research and Evaluation*, 223.

There are clear limitations to such a study. The first was the obvious fact that my researchers and I were situated in an evangelical Christian, largely Protestant, theological seminary. My own specialty is the relation of theology and culture, especially religion and the visual arts, and most of the researchers were students in various areas of Christian theology. This meant that we approached our Buddhist and Muslim neighbors as outsiders, on the one hand, and not as specialists in comparative religion, on the other. To avoid obvious infelicities and misunderstandings, our protocols were edited with assistance of various Muslim and Buddhist consultants. In order to get at corresponding practices these colleagues helped us phrase our questions appropriately.

But the real problem was how we, as Christians, could properly understand what our respondents were telling us. We approached this in two principal ways. One was our preference (which we also followed in the Christian study) for open-ended questions that allowed respondents to answer in ways they felt comfortable with, taking the conversation to places that appeared important to them. The student researchers became skilled in asking appropriate follow-up questions to clarify things they did not understand, and respondents generously took time to explain what their answers meant. This resulted in interviews that were typically much longer than the Christian interviews had been—they frequently extended beyond the hour limit we had set for ourselves, and the transcripts, some stretching to twenty or twenty-five single-spaced pages, provided us with a richly textured picture of these religious worlds.

But the other adjustment we made was to think about our work, and to write up our findings, as a conversation between the Christian author (and researchers) and the voices from these neighboring faiths. In this way, rather than ignoring the differences, we sought to take advantage of them and use the diversity to enrich the study. Where certain things puzzled us, I have commented on this; where other things surprised us, I have sought to understand why. In the conclusion I have tried to bring the three traditions together and provide a window on the differences and similarities among these traditions, with respect to ritual, visual elements, and belief. It would be a mistake then to claim this is a straightforward study of religious practices and visual elements of Buddhism and Islam; it is rather a Christian inquiry into these things and a conversation about the different aesthetics that emerge. Though specialists in Buddhist or Muslim practices may not find anything new or striking, it is hoped the comparative perspective may sometimes be illuminating.

Given its ethnographic character, the study is descriptive rather than normative. That is, we asked respondents to describe their actual experience of meditation or prayer, rather than their beliefs about these things. As any researcher knows, it is not possible to separate these completely. Frequently, respondents would preface their answers with a recognition that "Buddhists/Muslims believe or think that . . ." But they would just as often go on to describe what they usually did or how they ordinarily responded—sometimes in some contrast to what their traditions had taught them.

Since we were interested in what is typical and customary in these traditions, we watched for common expressions and recurring motifs that suggested shared values. Differences intruded, obviously, between immigrant and American-born Buddhists, for example, or between Sunni and Shia Muslims, and we will comment on these when they seems significant. But we wanted to see whether and to what extent these world faiths maintain their traditional foci in the multicultural and pluralistic environment of Southern California, and how these traditional elements issue in a particular aesthetic of practice that might be compared to that of Christians.

This goal might appear to leave us open to the accusation of simplifying (or essentializing) what are in fact highly complex and diverse faiths. Scholars are justifiably suspicious of global claims about what Buddhism or Islam "teaches," especially when this is expressed in categorical terms. In the present case, when we began the research, we did not necessarily assume consistency among the various temples and mosques—in some cases we actually expected and looked for differences that others had called to our attention. After all our setting is a highly pluralistic city and Buddhism and Islam are immigrant faiths that come from a variety of settings. But in the event, a coherent profile of feelings and attitudes emerged in the course of the interviews, which I have tried to capture in this book. While we soon became aware of the diversity—generational or cultural—that exists, this did not keep our sample from expressing a fairly consistent view of the practices and objects that we wanted to study. It is no doubt true that we missed nuances of differences that respondents were expressing, and this surely deserves further attention, but overall we were surprised by the commonality among the responses. Exploring in more detail the differences among these groups would entail a further study that would ask a different set of questions. While Shia and Sunni believers generally share a Muslim imagination, for example, exploring ways their visual cultures and ritual practices differ would be an entirely appropriate line of research. That however is work we do not attempt here.

As non-specialists we felt it appropriate, for the most part, to interview ordinary members of these communities—only two of eight at each site were leaders. This is especially fitting given that in both faiths the line between professional and lay leadership is not always clearly drawn. So this is a study of vernacular views of religious practice—what might be called common Buddhism and common Islam, and not a study of normative Buddhism and Islam. We wanted to learn what ordinary Buddhists and Muslims share in common. The brief synopses of these faiths in the introduction is meant only to orient readers to the general development of these traditions, and their attitudes toward art and the visual in particular, not to suggest any normative history that informed our research questions. In this descriptive study then I have sought to draw a picture of these faiths as they are lived and performed, what in the Christian tradition has been called "primary theology"—that is the theology of the basic practices of prayer, confession, praise, and so on. This also influenced our preference for the language of "meaning" rather than "truth" in describing the faiths. That is we were interested in the experience and reception of faith rather than its historical or normative character. While this perspective will perhaps puzzle (especially) some Christian readers, the justification for it will become clear in the course of the study.

As a further limitation we have focused on the visual or sensory culture of these religious traditions. While some of the questions we asked were more general in nature, the majority centered on visual elements, ritual practice and spatial arrangements, that provide the particular focus for this (and the previous) study. We explain and defend this approach in the introduction, but here let me say that I have been motivated in this by two concerns. First, my own interest in religion and the arts has led me to believe that aesthetic factors are often more important to religious believers (as to nonbelievers) than is usually recognized—and indeed are becoming increasingly salient in our media saturated and aesthetically aware culture. This claim is, in part at least, an empirical one, and so a focus on visual culture provided an appropriate means to explore this hypothesis.[5] Secondly, it

5. I develop this thesis about contemporary culture in Dyrness, *Poetic Theology: God*

seemed to me, that asking about the physical environment and the practices that animate this space, provided a fresh angle for the larger project of interfaith encounter—which has become increasingly ramified and enriched in the last decade. Perhaps we can come to a deeper mutual understanding by reflecting on, and comparing, cherished practices and aesthetic objects, than we can by studying texts or statements of belief alone.

So this small study is offered as a kind of first step in the direction of what I am calling interfaith aesthetics. While this is done against the backdrop of the great aesthetic traditions of these two faiths, the focus here is more modestly on the everyday religious practices of believers in their search to make something beautiful of their lives. My colleagues and I offer it as little more than a proposal that might be framed as follows: treasuring our ordinary (religious) lives together, especially our places of worship (or of meditation) and their visual culture, might be as good a way of getting acquainted as other more grand or powerful proposals that are on offer in the larger culture.

This study would not have been possible without the cooperation of a large group of colleagues, both in and outside of Fuller Seminary. First of all we are deeply indebted to all the many friends who agreed to be interviewed by strangers and who often offered hospitality beyond what we expected—searching for pictures or prints, offering warm welcome, and even in several cases a hot drink or meals. (These respondents have been given pseudonyms in the study; only leaders, as public figures, are named.) In the Muslim community we could not have proceeded without the generous partnership of the Shura Council of Southern California and its executive director, and our dear friend, Shakeel Syed. Beyond this Dr. Sadegh Namazikhah of Imam Center in Palms, Usman Madha of King Fahad Mosque in Culver City, Naim Shaw of Masjid Ibad Allah, and Yassir Fazaga of the Islamic Foundation of Southern California were all generous partners in arranging visits and interviews. Sumaya Abubaker, of the Center for Religion and Civic Culture at USC, served as a consultant for the project as well as conducting a number of interviews. Hirokazu Kosaka, artistic director of the Japanese Cultural and Community Center in Little Tokyo was a valued consultant who helped us connect with Buddhist temples. Vibul Wonprasat of Wat Thai Temple in North Hollywood opened doors for us, as did Mary Stancavage at Against The Stream, a Buddhist study center. The photographs are by Whitney Warnes, who became an essential and

---

and the Poetics of Everyday Life, chapter 1.

valued part of our team. The real heroes of the project were the student researchers from Fuller: April Alkema, Nicholas Barrett, Jane Prior Gillespie, Jenny Jedlinsky, Darren Schlack, Jordan Schumacher, and senior researchers Dr. Mareque Steele Ireland and Leah Buturain Schneider. Keeping all these motivated, informed, and paid, were senior researcher and research coordinator Grete Gryzwana and Kathleen Tiemubol, operations manager in the Brehm office. Since the grant and study are conducted under the auspices of the Brehm Center for Worship and the Arts I am especially grateful to the former program director Lynn Reynolds and executive director Dr. Fred Davison who provided encouraging support throughout. I am further grateful for encouragement and advice from academic colleagues both in and outside of Fuller: Ellison Banks Findly, Cecilia Gonzalez-Andrieu, Mark Heim, Todd Johnson, Robert Johnston, Roberta King, Tanya Luhrmann, David Morgan, Joseph Prabhu, Sally Promey, and Duncan Williams. I am grateful to Kenneth George for helping obtain permission to use the work of Indonesian artist Abdul Dijalil Pirous. The study could not have begun without the warm encouragement and support of Michael Gilligan and Lynn Swazy at the Henry Luce Foundation; they have earned our deep gratitude. Dr. Chris Spinks, Justin Haskell, and Heather Carraher from Cascade Books, and my colleague Clay Schmit and my research assistant Shannon Proctor provided essential and competent support in seeing the book through the press and allowing it to be a part of the Brehm series on faith and art. Last but not least to my spouse, Dr. Grace Roberts Dyrness, who trained all the researchers and offered significant contacts from her huge group of friends in Los Angeles just when we needed them, I offer inadequate thanks and much love.

December, 2011
San Jose, Costa Rica

Introduction

Until recently the study of religion in Western theological schools and departments of religion has focused mainly on written texts—students' education has consisted largely of reading religious texts and writing their own commentaries in the form of additional texts. Meanwhile the exposure of most people to religions other than their own is more likely to be via aesthetic or ritual objects and practices. Many people have seen Buddhist sculptures in a museum, or have heard a Muslim call to prayer while traveling; very few have any exposure to the Quran, to say nothing of ancient Pali texts.

This disconnect is the occasion, though not the object of this study. Given its nature as an ethnographic study of the Buddhist and Muslim experience of devotion, especially of its visual and ritual elements, it is appropriate to begin with a recognition of this divide. I am struck by the fact that while many academics find this text-based approach congenial, ordinary people often find it strange. Theologian Roberto Goizeuta, for example, describes the dissatisfaction many religious people, especially from minority cultures, feel with such traditional approaches. For the U.S. Hispanic Catholic, he notes:

> . . . it will not be sufficient to read books about Jesus Christ, or even study relevant dogmatic declarations or biblical texts—important as these might be. We must instead look first—even if not only—to the concrete, historical relationship to Jesus (often for example by actually touching his image and kissing his feet); [it is here] that we come to know him, as it is in our concrete historical relationship with our families and friends that we come to know these.[1]

The religious identity of Hispanic Catholics, and, Goizueta points out, of many other communities, is constituted by the material world they

1. Goizeuta, *Caminemos con Jesus*, 54n12 and 168.

1

inhabit—the concrete relationships with family and friends, and the visual objects and practices that animate this world. Written accounts are not always the best entry way into this world.

To be sure, as Goizueta implies, there is much to be gained from the textual study of religion, but the more concrete expressions of religious belief such as processions and pilgrimages, or its music and images, for most believers, are surely just as important. Recent interreligious encounters are increasingly recognizing these other dimensions of faith, and this reflects changing attitudes toward the nature of religion itself.[2] Western definitions of religion have largely derived from the Reformation and later from Enlightenment philosophers, for whom belief and personal subjective experience were defining categories. A century ago anthropologists began studying concrete forms of religion but, initially at least, they continued to work in Western universalizing categories. As Talal Asad notes, what the West took as the transcendental essence of religion is actually the product of a unique post-Reformation history.[3] What this ignores, Asad believes, is the authorizing process at work in forming religious motivations. Medieval religion consisted of a specific discipline that formed such motivations, but since then, "from being a concrete set of practical rules attached to specific practices of power and knowledge, religion has come to be abstract and universalized."[4] Thus it is accepted that religion can be best captured in beliefs and dogmas that can be compared across cultures and times. Or at least so the Western discourse on religion has assumed.

As Asad implies, this emphasis has specific religious grounding in the Protestant Reformation. It is widely recognized that a major change in the relationship between belief and practice took place at the Reformation.[5] Whereas previously ritual performance was dominant, the Reformers emphasized right understanding over the right practice of ritual. As

2. Scholars of religion now commonly acknowledge this in theory if not in practice. Catherine Albanese's influential study proposed that religion consists of four dimensions: explanations of meaning (creeds); rules which govern behavior (codes); shared social institutions; and multisensory communal rituals that engage believers' bodies (what she calls cultuses) (*America*, 8–10).

3. Talal, *Genealogies of Religion*, 24–42.

4. Ibid., 42.

5. I have explored these changes in Dyrness, *Reformed Theology and Visual Culture: The Protestant Imagination from Calvin to Edwards*, especially chapter 4. On the growing importance of practice in a Christian context see Dykstra, *Growing the Life of Faith: Education and Christian Practice*; and Bass and Volf, *Practicing Theology Beliefs and Practices in Christian Life*.

Edward Muir put this, in the Middle Ages the laity were "simply to envision Christ elevated on the cross, whenever they saw the raised host. They were to adore, not think."[6] With the Reformation things were in some ways reversed. Using Muir's terms, one is tempted to say with some exaggeration, the laity were instructed to think and not adore. Practices continued, of course, pastors still performed baptisms and celebrated the Eucharist, but as Muir points out, the focus on the theology—the meaning of these, was so pronounced that the reformers stumbled when it came to describing what these practices *did*. Muir notes: "They struggled to resolve the tension between the meaning they thought they found in scripture and the experience they wanted to provide for believers by participating in a sacrament."[7]

Ann Taves has shown how this influenced what counted as "religion." Reformers tended to characterize Catholic practices and the discipline this represented as "magic," while they called their own practices "true religion." "This distinction," she argues, "in turn heightened the Protestant distinction between ritual and experience and led Protestants to valorize experience along with Scripture in determining what counted as authentically religious."[8]

The subsequent study of religion then has been marked by the emphases formed during this period. Enlightenment religion might be said to have rationalized Reformation strategies even as it marginalized other dimensions of religion. Anthropological study of religion in the last century has consequently privileged belief over practice. This is reflected, for example, in the influential definition of religion formulated by Clifford Geertz in 1973, which has dominated subsequent approaches to religion. His focus was on religion as a "system of symbols," which, as he put it, formulated "conceptions of a general order of existence and clothing these conceptions with such an aura of factuality that the moods and motivations seem uniquely realistic."[9] Notice that the conceptions of religion are determinative and the outward forms in which these are clothed are somewhat less real. As a definition of religion this is not wrong so much as biased toward his own particular (Western and Christian) tradition of religion. This critique has been made by Asad and others after him.[10] But as Bruce

6. Muir, *Ritual in Early Modern Europe*, 172.

7. Ibid., 179.

8. Taves, *Religious Experience Reconsidered*, 147.

9. Geertz, "Religion as a Cultural System," 90.

10. In addition to Asad see Mahmood, *The Politics of Piety*.

Lincoln points out, it is not accidental that those voicing this critique have been students of Islam, for whom the dimensions of religion marginalized during the Reformation are central.[11] These differences became especially evident (and salient) in the comparative study represented in these pages.

The conclusion Ann Taves draws from this is to reject all "stipulated definitions" of religion, which she thinks artificially stabilize religious experience, and instead, to focus attention on the "process whereby people decide on the meaning of events and decide what matters most."[12] Taves thinks we ought to leave the defining of religion to the actors themselves, while developing what she calls an "ascriptional model" whereby we seek to learn how people come to consider something special or religious.[13] This fits with the general tendency to focus ethnographic work on the agency of the people and it has been the practice we have followed in our methodology.[14] Helpful as this is, however, it fails to illumine how these experiences are authorized over time—that is how religious traditions and communities are formed, and the specific role of discipline in shaping attitudes and motivations.[15] An interfaith interlocutor will be alert to both what people value in their religious practice and the practices that over time have provided a communal discipline, which in turn both forms communities and builds tradition.

Religious traditions represent patterns of communal life that are formed over long periods of time, and persist in recognizable ways. This happens because, as Asad notes, forms of practices become enduring disciplinary matrices. People learn these through imitation and example, but also through specific training and mentoring. The roll of tradition has often been overlooked in the study of religion in America, since the individual religious agent is usually the subject of study. Our studies have amply confirmed the continuing impact of these disciplinary matrices, even in the individualist culture of Southern California. At the same time they have

11. Lincoln, *Holy Terrors*. I am indebted to the discussion of Stambach, *Faith in Schools*, 75, for this reference.

12. Taves, "Religion in the Humanities," 291.

13. She calls these "composite ascriptional formations" (Taves, *Religious Experience*, 9–10).

14. See on this change of focus, Ortner, *Anthropology and Social Theory*.

15. There is still the image of the unattached agent choosing and evaluating experiences, and constructing a religious self. The assumption is that choice is intrinsically good. But as Asad points out, for monks in the monastery, "virtuous desire had first to be created *before* a virtuous choice could be made" (*Genealogies*, 126, emphasis added).

found that these received patterns of practice are freely (and sometimes creatively) appropriated by members of the tradition. Michael Partridge explains the interaction of these elements: "Each person lives their own 'particularized version' of the tradition. In turn, each affects and helps to shape the tradition . . . And the traditions do much to form particular people; and continue, throughout their lives, to provide the forms in which they can live particular lives."[16] In our study we have sought to keep in view both the traditional formation and the individual appropriation.

Sharing Matters of the Heart

If it is true that most people's experience of religion is in terms of the more visible and concrete aspects of faith, especially their aesthetic artifacts, it follows that an important dimension of interfaith encounter is embodied. This suggests that interfaith encounters should ideally include the sharing of the embodied experiences of religious images and practices, alongside conversations about the meaning of these. This further implies that an appropriate ethnography leads not only to shared awareness of meaning, but even to a kind of shared bodily knowledge—as when researchers sit with Buddhist respondents while they meditate or kneel with Muslims at prayer.[17]

In previous research focusing on the visual elements of Christian and Jewish practice, my colleagues and I have identified distinct religious imaginations that are characteristic of religious traditions.[18] I have earlier defined these as "the way people give shape to their world, in particular through the images and practices that express this shape . . . [and] that is a characteristic way of laying hold of the world and of God."[19] These are similar, in the religious sphere, to what Charles Taylor calls "social imaginaries." By this he means the way ordinary people imagine their social (or, in our case, their religious) surroundings, which is mostly framed not in theoretical terms, "but is carried in images, stories and legends."[20] Such symbolic ob-

16. Partridge, "Performing Faiths," 77.

17. For an excellent description of the bodily knowledge attendant on phenomenological ethnography see Nabhan-Warren, "Embodied Research and Writing," 378–407.

18. See Dyrness, *Senses of the Soul*. A PhD student and Luce Senior Researcher, Leah Buturain Schneider has recently completed a similar study of Jewish practices, which she has organized under the trope of "choreography."

19. Dyrness, *Reformed Theology and Visual Culture*, 6.

20. Taylor, *Modern Social Imaginaries*, 23.

jects and practices are critical because they express mostly implicit, though deep-seated communal commitments. In the terms of St. Augustine, the fifth-century Christian theologian, they reflect not what a person knows but what she loves. Or as Rumi the Sufi poet has written: "The value of a human being can be measured by what he or she most deeply wants. Be free of possessing things. Sit at an empty table. Be pleased with water, the taste of being at home."[21]

The enormous influence of Rumi on people outside the Muslim community illustrates the potential of aesthetics and art for interreligious encounter. Of course imagery can produce conflict, as in the Danish cartoon episode, and it can incite divisions, as Islamist art has done in Iran.[22] But historically the encounter between religious aesthetic traditions has been mostly positive and mutually enriching. Though it is difficult to be precise, there is surely some relation between the classical Greek image of the human form and the development of the Buddha image in the Gandharan style.[23] In addition one might reflect on the well-known influence of Moorish architecture on the Gothic cathedral,[24] the tenth-century Christian adaptation of Buddhist and Daoist liturgy, or surviving images of Christian worshipers in the form of Bodhisattvas.[25] Archbishop Marcello Zago, formerly Secretary for Evangelization in the Vatican, has summed up the importance and potential of such mutual exposure: "Almost of necessity we share in some expression of other's experience, connected with the stages of human existence, such as birth, marriage death and socio-religious festivals. Sharing can also lead to more intimate experiences such as forms of prayer and meditation, though it is . . . [not] possible to enter into the heart of the religion itself. It is possible to go from knowledge of the forms and content of the experiences to sharing them."[26] The knowledge of the ritual objects and practices of others implies more than historical or theoretical information; it must include a thick description of the function and experience of these by the adherents themselves. The voices of respondents, which form the heart of this book, provide hints of such an embodied and lived perspective.

21. Rumi, *The Glance*, 85.

22. See Kamrane, "Le Transcendent au service de l'immanent," 54.

23. See Ch'En. *Buddhism;* and Coomaraswamy, "The Origin of the Buddha Image."

24. Burckhardt, *Sacred Art in East and West*, 144.

25. See Loverance, *Christian Art*.

26. Zago, "The New Millennium," 12.

Enriching the Interfaith Conversation

Encounters with people of a different faith have become a fact of life for a growing number of people, both in Europe and North America. In academia an earlier focus on comparative religion has developed into a finer scrutiny carried out from within various religious communities. This has issued in two movements worthy of note, the one called comparative theology and another scriptural reasoning.[27] Given the increasing proximity of religions to each other, a closer reading of neighboring faiths has become necessary—one that attends to and respects their differences. Both these movements are important for our purposes because they aim to study faith traditions not from the outside but, as it were, from within. Francis Clooney describes the discipline of comparative theology as "the practice of rethinking aspects of one's own faith tradition through the study of aspects of another faith tradition." This practice assumes that theology, while particularly characteristic of the Christian tradition, because of widely shared human commonalities can be described and studied comparatively across different religious traditions. "As an intellectual project," Clooney goes on, "theology is composed of intellectual practices that can be recognized by intelligent believers in multiple traditions."[28]

A good example of this comparative exercise is a recent study of "atonement" in Buddhist and Christian traditions, by a Christian theologian Mark Heim.[29] Heim proposes to look at the dynamics of atonement by asking how Christ and the Bodhisattvas fulfill this dynamic in their respective traditions. Both involve historical events—the cross in one case and the spiritual practice of the Bodhisattvas in the other. By a careful study of Christian and Buddhist texts he seeks to show how both these historical events became a "field of merit" that changed the objective environment in which suffering is addressed. Such reflections, for Heim as a Christian theologian, shed new light on the moral influence theory of the atonement in Peter Abelard, and more generally, on the cross as a social event. He wants to broaden Christian understandings of the atonement by asking, not, how is this is to be understood? but what social practices does it entail?

A further example of comparative study has taken place within the academy between Christian, Jewish, and Muslim scholars, focusing on

27. See the description of these developments in Locklin and Nicholson, "The Return of Comparative Theology," 479–514.

28. Clooney, "Comparative Theology," 654, and see 660.

29. Heim, "Sharing Tensions."

what they call comparative scriptural reasoning.[30] These conversations are attempts to read sacred texts within a framework of friendship and hospitality and with an openness to various media, cultures, and disciplinary approaches. As David Ford notes, since some of the bitterest encounters between faiths involves an appeal to "scripture," and given that any attempt to confront the "core identity of any of these faiths will inevitably involved its scriptures," forming small interfaith groups of scholars dedicated to careful listening and mutual learning would appear to be a worthy project.[31] David Ford summarizes the hopes for these discussions: "The condition for wise Abrahamic practicality is that each tradition allows itself to have its own wisdom questioned and transformed in engagement with the others. This means recognizing them as analogous wisdoms with the potential of worthwhile interplay . . . [comprising] a joint response by Jews, Christians and Muslims, inspired by the reading of their scriptures, to the cries of a suffering world."[32]

Interactions like these have done much to deepen mutual understanding and, indeed, to enrich practitioners on both sides of the exchange. These programs represent a significant development in the academic study of religion, wherein religious convictions are examined from within faith communities, rather than studied objectively by outsiders. In this respect, the present study follows a similar pattern. But in spite of the professed desire of both to expand discussions to include historical and social events in the case of Heim, and aesthetic and liturgical practices in the case of Ford, the discussion usually furthers a project that is fundamentally intellectual (though both would want to resist this). Much is to be gained from this, of course, but it risks leaving out of account, or at least reifying, the lived world of ordinary religious people. In the end, the object of study and comparison is still various kinds of religious texts. What if the focus were broadened to include the practices and conceptions of ordinary people in the course of their religious life? More to the point what if attention was paid, not only to what the practices might *mean*, important as this is, but to what they *do* for people—how people feel and respond to them, and what the consequences of this might be for their lives? That is, what if our focus was not on *what* but *how* people believe?

---

30. See Ford, *Christian Wisdom*.

31. Ibid., 276.

32. Ibid., 299 and 303.

This larger embodied faith is the intended focus of this study. The methodology of the project was originally conceived as a study of visual culture. The methodology of visual culture seeks to understand communities, not in terms of their beliefs, but by means of their material and visual culture, specifically their images and ritual practices, that embody their faith. Further it seeks to understand how these impact believers. David Morgan has defined visual culture as the study of the visual mediation of religious belief.[33] He proposes a focus on visual culture because it "concentrates on the work that images do in constructing and maintaining . . . a sense of order in a particular place and time."[34] In this method of approach (Morgan thinks, at this time, this is more of a method than a field of study), one seeks not to explain the picture or practice—the common practice of iconographical and ritual studies—but to describe what this does, how the person puts this to work in their lives. For this transaction to take place—this putting-faith-to-work—Morgan argues, people develop various interpretive schemes, or "epistemological lenses,"[35] that are widely shared—what we are calling religious imaginations.

While this methodology has been helpful, in the course of the interviews it became clear that a focus on visual elements was artificial and, in some cases and for a variety of reasons, impossible. Even when questioned about imagery, respondents tended to focus not on individual images but on how these produced or allowed meaning in the larger context of the religious experience. In fact scholars have come themselves to recognize the need for more comprehensive categories. Visual culture itself was an attempt to enlarge the scope of explanatory factors in religion, to move beyond the word-oriented approach to a more holistic conception of the religious experience. That approach recognized that images and the visual always accompany verbal proclamation and, in addition to interacting with verbal elements, carry their own cognitive weight.[36] But, in our study, we found that this weight is enhanced or diminished by the context and expectations that believers bring to that context. Moreover this weight was often allied with other sensory aspects of what might be called the aesthetics of worship, forming in the process complex embodied and performed images. In fact scholars have more recently begun to recognize this holistic

33. Morgan, *The Sacred Gaze*, 6.
34. Ibid., 29.
35. Ibid., 105.
36. See Freedberg, *The Power of Images*.

character and are now speaking of sensory culture, rather than visual culture, as the more appropriate and comprehensive focus.[37]

This focus on the role of environment and aesthetic factors in religious experience assumes that the religious faith of most people is to a greater or lesser extent tacit rather than explicit. It involves activities and objects that are often deeply moving and influential but which might be only imperfectly understood—or indeed not *consciously* understood at all. The importance of practice in the understanding of faith has come to be widely understood. But as we have noted, the bias of belief (and subjective experience) over practice continues to be influential. This confusion is significant, I want to argue, because it often blinds Christian thinkers to the influence (and the potential) of their own ritual practice and, equally significant, the differing potential to be found in the practice of other faiths. The difference between traditions in the balance between practice and meaning appeared time and again in the interviews, and the varying evaluations of these will be a major theme addressed in the conclusion.

Throughout the study the role of the body and embodiment were critical. Scholars recently have recognized that it is in various forms of participation, in a bodily and concrete sense, that people are formed by religious traditions and that they come to "know" their faiths. We have noted already the contribution of David Morgan. Building on the phenomenological tradition of philosophy, Mark Johnson and others have argued that our experience of embodiment in the space-time world actually makes possible our mental appropriation of that world. It is, Johnson thinks, the "structures of our bodily experience . . . [that] help to explain how anything . . . can be meaningful."[38] The structure that results from shared (and embodied) practices, he argues, comes to be widely held in traditional conceptions of what we call reason. Similarly, though working in a somewhat different tradition, Margaret Archer has argued that our basic orientation in the world provides raw materials and analogies from which we develop formal processes of reason. It is in measuring difference between the self and the natural world that we assess and express belief. She says: "The key to this differentiation lies in human powers of sight and movement (theory and practice)."[39] Among the practices that shape these worlds are

---

37. See Promey and Brisman, "Sensory Cultures."

38. Johnson, *The Body in the Mind*, 139. See also Dreyfus, *What Computers Still Can't Do*.

39. Archer, *Being Human*, 134. Our world, she thinks, is "earthed in the commonality

the interpretive visual practices that, in David Morgan's terms, become specific sites of religious belief—they become places "where belief happens."[40] If these scholars are right, then attention to the embodied practices and images of faith is essential, not only to interfaith endeavors, but also for a deeper awareness of one's own faith.

Interfaith Aesthetics?

So the whole complex of religious practice and belief, from ritual practice to meditation and contemplation, from the burning of incense to the ritual washing before prayers, will be the object of attention in this study. We will be interested in how these are experienced and lived out by the believer. But there is another aspect I want to highlight—what I am calling "interfaith aesthetics." When attention is paid to the visual and spatial elements of religion a further dimension emerges. Ritual practice and images, it turns out, not only serve as cognitive markers, but they regularly become aesthetic sites. That is what moves believers is not simply the truth or authenticity of a tradition, significant as these are, but what we might call the aesthetic surface of their communal life. When attention is paid to the holistic, embodied engagement with religious traditions, aesthetic responses come naturally. Our sample, when asked about specific images or ritual, regularly made reference to feelings of deep joy or rewarding solidarity with others. In other words, central to any religious practice is affective attraction that is triggered by various forms of sense and bodily experience. The importance of this dimension of religion means that what sparks desire and love is not marginal but central to religious motivation and practice.[41] Reflection on this affective dimension then, in the comparative study of traditions, might appropriately be called "interfaith aesthetics."

At first glance it might appear odd to characterize this visual and ritual dimension as aesthetic, since the objects and practices in question are frequently not formed with aesthetic intent. To be sure, much of the art in cultures influenced by these great religious traditions owes a deep historical debt to these living faiths, and some of the best art was formed directly for the cult. But it is not simply these classical forms that I have in

of embodied practices in the natural world" (135).

40. Morgan, *The Sacred Gaze*, 8.

41. This is the central conviction argued in my book *Poetic Theology: God and the Poetics of Everyday Life*.

mind; as I indicated I want to broaden the discussion of aesthetics beyond what we ordinarily think of as works of art, to the holistic and affective responsive of people in the practice of their faith. Here I have been influenced by the work of Roberto Goizueta. Working in the broad tradition of liberation theology, Goizueta argues that the true nature of the person is a "praxis" whose end is internal to itself and whose nature is intersubjective.[42] The key category for understanding human experience, Goizueta thinks, is not social transformation, as liberationists have argued, but aesthetic fusion—the former is often a by-product, but the latter constitutes the essence of human action (he is critical of liberation theology for allowing its functional goals to supplant the aesthetic). Learning from the Mexican philosopher Jose Vasconcelos, Goizeuta argues that true understanding involves an "empathic fusion" between subject and object that fosters the enjoyment and celebration of the object.[43] Human relationships invariably issue in aesthetic objects and practices that promote this fusion, and these become especially prominent in peoples' religious lives. It is this aesthetic dimension, where embodied symbols and practices spark delight, that I wish to highlight in the discussion that follows.

An Approach to Buddhist and Muslim Imaginations—a Christian Reading

Since we are analyzing a sample of Buddhist and Muslim respondents about the ordinary practice of their faith, we need to spend some time reflecting on these traditions. As we have said in the preface, our focus is on a vernacular as opposed to a normative construal of religious traditions. That is, we are not interested in how the trained leaders or standard texts describe the tradition so much as what people actually make of this. We seek to discover what we are calling *common* Buddhism and Islam. Still it might be useful to have some general outline of the tradition before us as we listen to the voices of these respondents. Though it is impossible here to give a complete picture these faiths, I will seek to sketch out some broadly accepted notions about, especially, visual culture in these traditions and its embodiment in their religious practices. In the remainder of this introductory chapter this will be our task.

---

42. Goizueta *Caminemos con Jesus*, 81–85.

43. Ibid., 91–92.

Buddhism

The Buddha (lit. "the awakened one") was the designation of the historical figure Guatama Siddhartha (ca. 566–486 BCE), who renounced his
princely inheritance and devoted himself to the spiritual life and the study
of spiritual practices, eventually achieving enlightenment or liberation
from the chain of human bondage. Traditionally Buddhists are those who
take refuge in the three jewels of saving reality: the Buddha, the Dharma,
and the Sangha.[44] The Buddha, or awakened one, refers not only to the historical Guatama, but to enlightened figures thought to precede and follow
him. Some branches of Buddhism posit many Buddhas living in various
places and times; most schools assert that there is a Buddha nature in all
sentient creatures, inclining them to a common goal. Dharma ("teaching")
refers to the message of the Buddha that he passed on to his disciples and
that is authoritatively preserved in the Sutras. The best known short form
of the Dharma is the four noble truths: life is suffering (dukkha); suffering
is caused by desire for the things of this life (the realm called "samsara");
suffering can be stopped by renouncing this desire (an ultimate goal called
"nirvana"); and, finally there is an eightfold path that assures the cessation
of suffering (right views, intention, speech, conduct, livelihood, effort,
mindfulness, and concentration). The Sangha refers to the community of
those who follow the Buddha and the Dharma. Strictly speaking in Buddhist tradition the Sangha refers to monks who have devoted themselves
to the noble path, but it is often extended to include all those who seek to
follow this path.

Historically Buddhism arose in the context of Hinduism as a kind of
reform movement—in fact it arose in the context of other ascetic movements in the sixth century BCE. As a result it cannot be understood apart
from the deep spirituality of Hindu culture, and, as we will note, it accommodated popular forms of the long dominant Hindu religiosity. Buddhism
soon developed into a so-called greater vehicle, termed Mahayana, and a
lesser vehicle, Hinayana, of which Theravada Buddhism is the most ancient
and, for our purposes, the most prominent. Mahayana Buddhism arose in
the context of stupa worship, which responded to the question of how to
conceive of Buddha's body after his death (a stupa is a cylindrical mound

---

44. This way of framing Buddhism is suggested by Yoshinori, *Buddhist Spirituality
I: Indian, Southeast Asian, Tibetan and Early Chinese*; and *Buddhist Spirituality II: Later
China, Korea, Japan and the Modern World*. Hereafter *BS I* and *BS II*. Cf. *BS I*, xvff, from
which this initial summary is drawn.

serving as a memorial). From very early times those gathering around Buddha stupas—memorials to the Buddha, began to form the first public face of Buddhist faith in the world (as opposed to the faith of the monks in the monasteries).[45] The most significant contribution of the Mahayana school is the notion of the Bodhisattva. If, as they believed, there have been many Buddhas before and after the Guatama, there could also be many aspirants to Buddhahood in any age. From this arose the notion of the Bodhisattva, one who was destined for enlightenment but postponed this for the sake of helping others pursue the way to liberation. This is described in one of the sutras as follows: "The Bodhisattva reflects, and pronounces this vow: 'I will become the light of the world, possessing the virtues of the Buddha—the ten powers, his omniscience. All sentient beings are burning in the flames of covetousness hatred, and confusion. I will rescue them all by extinguishing the suffering of the evil destinies.'"[46]

Theravada Buddhism, which spread into Southeast Asia in the first millennium of the Christian era, looked on itself as reforming the Mahayana tradition by recovering the original practices of Buddhist meditation—which were authoritatively preserved in the Pali canon (100 BCE to 100 CE).[47] This was elaborated in a famous fifth-century Sri Lankan text on "The Path to Purification" that has been influential up to this day. The steps laid out in this process are (1) Sila, which encompasses the ethical practices based on the basic precepts of Buddhism; (2) these are to be deepened, taken to heart, by meditation (Samadhi), which is a deep mental concentration on a given subject or object—a descent into oneself sometimes described as "enstasy" (as opposed to "ecstasy" or the movement to transcend oneself); (3) the final stage (Pañña) is liberating knowledge of the human existence freed from attachment to samsara.

Buddhism prospered in large part because wherever it went it accommodated itself synergistically to indigenous religious practices—a fact that characterizes Buddhism to this day. (Yoshinori argues that in contrast to Christianity there never were underground heretical movements, such as gnosticism, spiritism, and mysticism, which [in Christianity] were suppressed by the religious authorities.)[48] In Southeast Asia, Theravada Buddhism did not deny the existence of the local gods and spirits, though it

45. Yoshinori, *BS I*, 143.
46. Quoted by Luis O. Gómez in *BS I*, 163.
47. See Winston King, "Theravada in Southeast Asia" in *BS I*, 84–86, for what follows.
48. *BS I*, xxv.

did make them of lesser importance. They were reconceived as helpers to the Buddha and important benefactors in the worldly order. As Winston King notes, "Converts, thus able to keep their old gods and worship-magic patterns to some degree, found Buddhism superior but not strange and forbidding."[49] Theravada Buddhism is represented in our sample by the Wat Thai Temple in North Hollywood, and Against the Stream, an American Buddhist movement led by Noah Levine.

"Against the Stream"

Mahayana Buddhism, however, was to prove more adaptable to a wide variety of cultures. During the first millennium of the Christian era, it passed into Tibet and developed various esoteric divinities and practices. These are often portrayed on Tibetan thankas, which are religious images of divinities mounted on brocade and hung in temples or carried in religious processions. Tibetan Buddhism is represented in our sample by the Bodhi Path community in Pasadena. Mahayana Buddhism also entered China by the third century of the Christian era. Daoists at first recognized it simply as a variation of their own understanding of the nurture of human energies, a preconception that influenced the development of Buddhism in China.[50]

49. *BS I*, 85. He notes that another part of the success of Buddhism in Southeast Asia reflected the high esteem which Indian civilization enjoyed during this time.

50. For these insights, see Whalen Lai, "The Three Jewels in China," *BS I*, 275–81.

The Daoists at least had an idea of a spiritual core of reality that they called the Dao.

The encounter of Buddhism with Confucianism with its focus on social immortality was another matter entirely. Confucian scholars especially objected to the notion of "karma," the Buddhist (and Hindu) idea that injustice in one life would be addressed in another one. Confucians were persuaded that injustice would be redressed in some future adjustment of society. But these faiths—Daoism, Confucianism, and Buddhism—learned to coexist in China and grew to be the three religions most congenial to Chinese culture. In the end the mutual influence among these religions gave Buddhism a more this-worldly emphasis and a preoccupation with methods of attaining enlightenment. This stream of Mahayana Buddhism is represented in our study by the large Hsi Lai Temple in Whittier.

The emphasis on method is particularly characteristic of Ch'an Buddhism which passed from India into China early in the first millennium BCE, and eventually spread into Japan, where it is known as Zen (and where it eventually supplanted Shintoism as the state religion). In Zen, enlightenment is achieved by transmission from master to disciple, mostly without words or letters.[51] The essence of Zen, Philip Yampolsky says, "is in that singular moment of personal encounter wherein a master's insight touches the student's inherent purity of being."[52] This may result from some momentary intuition sparked by a gesture or some response on the part of the teacher. The student is forever changed from this experience and sees him/herself and the world from a new perspective. A further characteristic of this tradition is a focus on various forms of meditation deriving from various teachers, and the conviction that enlightenment can be achieved in this life—rather than occurring through a process of transmigration (or reincarnation) as in various forms of Theravada Buddhism. The sample of respondents from the Zen Soto mission in Little Tokyo is representative of this stream of Buddhist practice.

Meditation of various kinds and in a variety of forms is the dominant practice of Buddhism. Paul Griffiths describes meditation as "a self-conscious attempt to alter, in a systematic and thorough-going way, the practitioner's perceptual, cognitive and affective experience."[53] The goal of this practice is a spiritual orientation and a moral transformation rather than

51. See Philip Yampolsky "Ch'an," *BS II*, 3–32.

52. Ibid., 31.

53. "Indian Buddhist Meditation," *BS I*, 34 and 35.

cognitive insight into the nature of things. As G. C. Pande, puts it, Buddhist faith is "conative, not cognitive,"[54] involving more a discipline of the will rather than the exercise of the mind. But this is not to say external practices and imagery play no role. In the Indian tradition, Griffiths points out, meditative practices are intimately related to various forms of ritual and magic. The question we raise in this study is what relation, in our Southern Californian and American setting, do the practices of meditation (sometimes called simply "sitting") sustain with traditional ritual practices (often reflecting some form of popular religion) and imagery? How might the visual practices that have developed in this setting indicate (new) emerging interpretive schemes?

The most dominant and readily recognizable image in Buddhist communities is the Buddha himself in various poses and with different hand gestures (called "mudras")—references to this image are common among our respondents. In the earliest period it was forbidden to portray the Buddha, and his presence was symbolized by the Bodhi Tree (the supposed site of the Guatama's enlightenment), the wheel representing the Dharma, the footprint, or the stupa (the cylindrical memorial we referred to earlier)—symbols that continue to characterize Buddhist iconography. Around the time of Christ images of Buddha began to appear, stimulated perhaps by the iconography of the Southeast Asian and Chinese cultures into which the faith was migrating (one of the monks at Hsi Lai has expressed the hope that there would eventually be an American form of the Buddha!). There were both foreign and indigenous influences on the form the Buddha took. We mentioned above the supposition (controversial for some) that Greek images of Apollo may have been influential; Titus Burckhardt points out, however, that the Divine Man on a lotus derived from ancient Hindu iconography and this also influenced the form of the Buddha that finally appeared.[55]

54. *BS I*, 14.

55. See Burckhardt, *Sacred Art in East and West*, 163. See the recent challenge to this supposed "aniconic" period in Pal, *Buddhist Art*.

Chanting at Wat Thai Temple

The relation of the various images and symbols to Buddhist practice is complex and its history need not detain us here. On the one hand the various symbols speak importantly about the Buddha's absence and thus of the enduring iconoclasm that resides deeply within the tradition. Buddha cannot be portrayed because of the evanescence of samsara (and early proponents thought it introduced the notion of change into the Buddha nature). As one writer describes this: "Aniconic imagery continued to figure in Buddhist iconography like a deep grammar at the semantic core of Buddhism's language of vision."[56] On the other hand, imagery and symbols, and the presence (and absence) of Buddha are essential to the process of vision and contemplation that characterize Buddhism. Images of Buddha, for example, soon became popular in the Theravada tradition of Southeast Asia (which had earlier resisted them) so that "people had a concrete object of worship, vividly represented."[57] Here before them stood the Buddha: a concrete and peaceful exemplar of the pathway to release from suffering. In our reflection on the interviews of our sample we will explore contemporary forms of this tension. Images, they tell us, play a vital if not central role

56. Hall Yiengruksawan, "Buddha's Bodies and the Iconographical Turn in Buddhism," *BS II*, 395.

57. King, *BS I*, 85. He notes how the exemplary life of the sangha similarly served as an invitation to follow the noble path.

in their meditation. But, at the same time, neither images nor meditation can be understood alone, and both together contribute to what might be termed a Buddhist imagination.

The seated Buddha

Islam

The other tradition of this study, bears some resemblance to Buddhism in two respects: its aniconic nature and its attempt to escape from illusion of selfhood and the rule of the ego. In other ways its radical monotheism springing from the nomadic tribes in the deserts of Arabia has produced a spirituality that sharply contrasts with the easy tolerance and the cultural embrace of Buddhism. While Buddhism adapted to its environment as it migrated across Asia and around the world, Islam though clearly a world religion, has remained anchored to its origins in the Arabic Middle East.

Islam (lit. "submission") is rooted in the revelation of God in the Quran as this was revealed to the Prophet Muhammad. Like Guatama, Muhammad sought to reform the decadent spirituality he saw around him. But, unlike the Buddha, he is considered the last in a line of prophets rather than a spiritual founder of a religious path to enlightenment. Muhammad (570–633 CE), Muslims believe, was a direct descendent of the biblical Ishmael, the son of Abraham, who is also considered the father of the Jewish and Christian faiths. Thus Muhammad is thought to continue a line of revelation that includes Moses and Jesus (to whom the Quran refers in some detail).[58] During twenty-three years of his mission, the Quran was revealed to Muhammad by the angel Gabriel.

The Quran itself, as the voice of God, is more foundational to Islam than the Hebrew and Christian Scriptures are to Judaism and Christianity. The Quran is believed to embody the "nature and inner substance of the Prophet"[59]—the two share a spiritual singularity. Accordingly it represents the very presence of God in the world. The fundamental motif of Islam is oneness, a unity (tawhid) that is believed to be revealed in the life of Muhammad and spelled out in the Quran. Of the many schools of Islamic thought and practice that were to develop, two are by far the largest and most important. The Sunnis (lit. "one who is a traditionist") comprising some eighty percent of all Muslims, are those who follow strictly the sayings of the Prophet (contained in the Hadith) and the record of the actions of the Prophet (the Sunnah). As they like to say, Sunnis carefully follow principles not persons (as they accuse the Shi'ites of doing)—the principles that are said to express the teaching of the Prophet. From the Quran and the Hadith and Sunnah, four schools of Islamic law developed during the Middle Ages. These schools have developed their consensus of opinions and analogical deductions (called ijma and qiyas) that together with the three primary sources, make up what is known as Shariah law—instructions thought to definitively embody God's will for regulating human conduct. "It is considered the duty of every Sunni Muslim to spend his life according to the dictates of the Shariah as interpreted by learned men

---

58. The major sources for this discussion are Nasr, *Islamic Spirituality I: Foundations* (hereafter *IS I*); and *Islamic Spirituality II: Manifestations* (hereafter *IS II*). On Muhammad's life see Qasimi, *IS I*, 65–95; and Armstrong, *Muhammad*.

59. *IS I*, xix.

and the jurists."[60] All the mosques of our study, except the Imam Center, represent this larger branch of Islam.

The Quran is central to Muslim practice

Sufism is a mystical movement that arose in the Middle Ages, partly in response to the exoteric (or public) character of the four schools of law. Through its various esoteric practices Sufism explored the inner dimensions of Islam. Although it arose in the context of Sunni Islam it has adherents in other branches as well. The best known Sufi scholar and poet Jalal al-Din Rumi (1207–1273), whom we quoted earlier, is said to have explored the "wonders of love."[61] He sought to open up the unseen and spiritual world for people by revealing God's grandeur and describing what separates humans from union with God. His teachings recall those of the Buddha in proposing that the goal of life is escape from the ego. As William Chittick describes his aim: "Pain and heartache derive from our illusory selfhood and our distance from the Self. To pass beyond Wrath and reach the Mercy which is the source of all, we must escape from the ego and dwell in the heart."[62]

60. *IS I*, 152.

61. See William C. Chittick, *IS II*, 105–26.

62. Ibid., 124.

The Shi'ites (lit. "party of followers") represent the second largest body of Muslims in the world. These follow the sayings of the first twelve imams, as well as the Quran and the sayings of the Prophet. They are sometimes referred to as the partisans of Ali, who was the cousin of Muhammad and considered his successor, who with his eleven male descendents make up the Twelve Imams whose teachings Shi'ites revere. Shi'ites point to the many verses in the Quran that confer special blessings on the Prophet and his descendents who are both models of virtues believers are to follow and also the authoritative interpreters of the Quran. Thus they follow the teachings of these Imams, and honor them by making pilgrimages to their tombs on memorial holidays. This branch of Islam is represented in our sample by the Imam Center in Palms, which is also an Iranian cultural center (Islam in Iran is largely Shi'ite).

All branches of Islam share common principles of the faith: the unity of God (tawhid), the mercy of God that brought the world into being, Muhammad as the last of the prophets, the Quran as the final revelation of God to people, and the resurrection as the goal of life, when everyone will stand in judgment before God. But these principles do not make up a set of beliefs in the same way as Christian doctrine nor are they elaborated in a theology as in Christianity. An Islamic theology does exist (called "kalam") as a "science that bears responsibility of solidly establishing religious beliefs by giving proofs and dispelling doubts,"[63] but this does not represent the deepest spiritual and intellectual expressions of Islam. More important are the philosophical elaborations of the nature of God and reflections on the Quran—all of which can as easily take the form of poetry as abstract formulation. (Muslim law was often promulgated in the form of poetry—a fact that we will want to comment on below.)

This de-emphasis on theology stems from the central role and special nature of the Quran. It is not a revelation or teaching about God so much as a recitation of the voice of God (Al-Qur'an means literally "recitation"). It has been called a "sonoral revelation." As Seyyed Nasr says, "Muslims live in a space defined by the sound of the Quran."[64] The voice of God through the angel Gabriel was believed to fill the sky and thus define the cosmos in which God's people lived. It is often likened more to the Christian understanding of Christ's incarnation than to the Jewish Torah or the Christian Bible.

---

63. *IS II*, 396.

64. Nasr in *IS I*, 4.

The Quran influences the forms and images characterizing Islamic worship in a variety of ways. The characteristic call to prayer is a chanting of Quranic verses; the prayers themselves, sung in the mosque, are derived from the Quran; the calligraphy on the walls is likely to include the name of Muhammad, and of God (Allah), along with messages from the Quran. Indeed the highest spiritual exercise is memorization of large portions of the Quran—in some cases even the whole of it! The practices that order Muslim life are oriented around the call, the prayers and recitation, fasting and pilgrimage. These are all rooted in the Quran.

The unity of Islam is meant to be its central characteristic, expressive as it is of the oneness of God, and the unity of the house of Islam (the Umah) across the world. But it is also reflected in the changelessness by which its history is read—both Sunnis and Shi'ites seek this continuity, albeit in different ways. Muhammad is the last prophet; the Quran is the final revelation. As a result Muslims are proud that they have needed no reformation. (I recently heard the famous progressive Muslim scholar Tariq Ramadan of Oxford University argue that Islam did not need to be reformed, rather the mind of Muslims needed to be re-formed by the tradition.) This unity is expressed in the fact that all Muslims read the same Quran in Arabic, they hear the same calls to prayer and Quranic recitations. They live and are formed in a common aural world—even if many respondents in our sample confess they understand little of what they hear.

The five pillars that define Islam are meant to image and enact the unity the believer is to live out in his or her life. They are the profession of faith (Shahada), "There is no God but Allah, and Muhammad is his prophet"; the five daily prayers, and the prayers in the mosque (Salat) with its attendant rituals of cleansing; the pilgrimage to Mecca (called the Hajj) at least once in one's lifetime for those who can afford it; fasting (Sawm), especially during the month of Ramadan; and finally, almsgiving (Zakat), originally a religious tax that is tied to and expressive of the efficacy of prayer. (The exertion necessary to love others and become selfless—or Jihad, which, as a last resort, might include violence to defeat enemies of this holy struggle, is sometimes considered a sixth pillar.) All of these practices are intended to express the oneness of God and the believer's total submission to this singular will. Each time one stands with bent head and arms crossed, or prostrates oneself during prayer, one expresses the annihilation of the self before God. The ablutions represent the need for cleansing and forgiveness in order to realize this oneness. The proper dress and specific instructions for almsgiving, pilgrimage, and life in general all give external expression to the internal purity of intention.[65]

Prayers at Masjid Ibadallah.

The oneness is also represented, spatially and structurally, by the mosque. Though taking various shapes, this structure is usually a single undifferentiated space for the community to gather, to study the Quran, and to pray. Often decorated with flowing calligraphy and patterned carpets, the mosque is also an image of paradise, an enclosed garden with its fountain for purifying the faithful. Titus Burckhardt quotes a description of the Hagia Sophia in Istanbul. It has no ascending or descending tendencies, as in Gothic cathedrals: "It is by its immobility that the atmosphere of a mosque is distinguished from all things ephemeral . . . In this architecture the beyond is not merely a goal, it is lived here and now, in a freedom exempt from all tendencies; there is a repose from all aspirations; its omnipresence is incorporated in the edifice so like a diamond."[66]

Mosques are also unified in their singular orientation toward Mecca. Believers are always expected to pray toward Mecca where lies the most sacred of all spaces, the Kabah.

65. See on these practices Syed Ali Ashraf, "The Inner Meaning of the Islamic Rites: Prayer, Pilgrimage, Fasting, Jihad" *IS I*, 111–30.

66. He is quoting U. Vog-Göknil in *IS II*, 523.

The Kabah, according to Islamic tradition, was built by Abraham as the first house of God on earth—the first mosque. Abraham's supposed travel to the spot represents the first pilgrimage, and it is the object of all Muslims' pilgrimage to this day. The Quran records God's charge to Abraham to "proclaim unto men the pilgrimage, that they may come unto thee on foot and on every lean camel out of every deep ravine"[67] (Quran 22:26–27). By the time of Muhammad, idols had been erected around the Kabah and its walls were covered with pictures. Muhammad personally saw to it the idols were removed and the images on the walls erased—though, interestingly, images of the virgin and Jesus were spared.[68] Now the faithful travel to Mecca on airplanes, but they still make the seven circular journeys around the Kabah on foot, amidst the sea of faithful.

Mosque at the Orange County Islamic Foundation.

These values and practices determine the role that art can play in the tradition and they also define what is forbidden. The strict monotheism of Islam and Muhammad's own struggle with polytheism has given the tradition an iconoclastic temper: no pictures of the God or the Prophet,

67. Unless otherwise noted, all quotations from the Quran are from *The Message of the Quran: The Full Account of the Revealed Arabic Text accompanied by Parallel Transliteration*, translated by Muhammad Asad.

68. *IS I*, 88.

nor indeed of any human figure, are allowed in the mosque, and images in general are given no positive role in worship. Such imaging practices, it is thought, attempt to project something absolute (God's unity) onto a relative object, and thus are always forbidden. Still it would not be accurate to say that art and beauty play no role in the religious tradition—quite the contrary, art has even been called by Seyyed Nasr a "second revelation," though it must be put in its proper Quranic context: "Islamic art, which may be called 'the second Revelation' of Islam, is rooted in the Quran, not in its outward form or as a result of applying explicit instructions contained in the Text but in its inner reality."[69]

Art plays this role insofar is it is a projection into the visual realm of the unity of God. Since it is based on and seeks to reflect this unity, Burckhardt notes, art must of necessity be abstract. And since it grows from the Quran, it must also be based on the physicality of the Arab language—its rhythm, its geometry and its light. Calligraphy, in its variety of beautiful forms, predominates in the visual arts, just as poetry dominates literature. Like the Quran itself, art's arabesque and interlacement are meant to encourage a dynamic (rather than a static) contemplation.[70] The iconoclasm of Islam is thus meant to be a positive rather than a negative characteristic: it encourages the faithful to see and project God's unity and lyrical play in everything—especially in the world of nature and the floral design of Muslim calligraphy. Burckhardt says "the luxuriance of typically Arab poetry lies in mental verbal arabesque and not in the profusion of images evoked."[71] For it is always possible that images might detract from the unified play of light and sound and from the contemplation these encourage. Islamic art then serves a religious end; it is finally about shaping an environment for the religious believer. All this explains why architecture plays such an important role in the Islamic tradition, a fact I will return to frequently in the discussion that follows.

69. *IS I*, 8.

70. See *IS II*, 514.

71. *IS II*, 514.

Verbal Arabesque at Imam Center

As I have said this study focuses on Buddhism and Islam and not directly on *Christianity*. But since it grows out of a study of Christian use of art and imagery and is done by Christians in a confessional setting, the Christian point of view must be readily acknowledged. While some might view the Christian perspective as a serious handicap, my colleagues and I have decided to look on it as an opportunity. The larger project into which this fits, after all, is that of interfaith dialogue and encounter. So, to foster comparison and mutual understanding, we have used the same protocol in these interviews that were used in Christian interviews—adapted to the different religious realities where that became necessary. And when writing up the results of our study, I decided to frame it as a discussion between a Christian observer and the various respondent voices. Where appropriate I have compared Buddhist or Islamic practices to Christian ones and, when something struck me as a Christian, I have registered my surprise or puzzlement. Because the Christian study has appeared in print, I will not here recount the results.[72] Though in order to foster a deeper conversation, I will make some extended reference to these in the conclusion. I postpone this discussion for a single reason: much that I want to discuss did not arise in the course of the Christian study, but only became evident when comparing this with what Muslim and Buddhists had to say. This of course

72. See Dyrness, *Senses of the Soul.*

is as it should be. We do, after all, have notions of difference before any deep engagement with other faiths, but even a casual encounter with others reveals how mistaken, even prejudicial, our assumptions often are.

What Does the California Setting Mean for Islam and Buddhism?

Before turning to the discussion of particular communities, I want to say something about the special setting in Southern California. On the one hand this provided a particularly rich opportunity to sample the many temples and mosques that are characteristic of immigrant communities in this urban center home to 13 million people. At the same time it raised the question of how and in what way the cultural and religious pluralism of this region impacted these communities. Outside of basic demographic information our protocol did not include questions comparing their religious experience in America with other places but the issue arose frequently and it deserves some attention here.

While the vast majority of our respondents would carry American passports, all of them participate in faiths that are commonly called immigrant religions. And since 9/11 the religious character of immigrants has received increasing scrutiny. Immigrants of course are not unusual in the United States, which is known as a nation of immigrants; and they are especially common in Southern California where one in three persons are foreign-born.[73] Our sample of Buddhist communities included persons born in ten different countries mostly from within Asia; those representing Islam were born in twelve countries, mostly from the Middle East, South Asia, and Africa. These often proudly commented on their ethnic background, confirming the finding of Peggy Levitt that "immigrants don't trade in their home country membership cards for an American one but belong to several communities at once."[74]

As one might expect from our brief introduction, Islam seemed the most resistant to alteration by its Southern California setting. In one case, the Imam Center, the mosque serves also as a cultural center, providing activities and language classes for Iranian immigrants. But mostly mosques served a variety of ethnic groups— a surprising result of our interviews (at least to us) was the discovery that believers often went to more than one

73. The figures are for Los Angeles County, see Miller et al., "Religious Dimensions," 101.

74. Levitt, *God Needs No Passport*, 2.

mosque to pray. From our sample it appears that the Muslim communities have been less successful than the Buddhist in attracting native-born Americans to their worship. The notable and important exception is the IbadAllah mosque, which includes a number of African American converts to Islam. Other mosques include many who have found a renewed faith since moving to America, and I will comment on these later. But all of the Muslims we surveyed, native-born and immigrant, practiced the faith in a similar way.

Buddhists in our sample displayed a much greater variety. Among the Buddhist temples were those that serve as a community center for their homeland—such as Wat Thai Temple in North Hollywood serving the Thai community, and the Zen Soto Mission in little Tokyo. Another, the Hsi Lai Temple in Whittier, which is the largest Buddhist temple in the Western hemisphere, served a more general role of bringing together worshipers from various ethnic groups, especially from Asia. Two, Bodhi Path and Against the Stream, were composed of mostly American converts to Buddhism—though there were commonly converts in the other sites as well. The success of Buddhism in adapting to the American environment is not a new characteristic of this faith, as we have seen, but it revealed a particular profile in our study that calls for some comment.

The voices of our Buddhist respondents displayed a striking diversity. In contrast to Islam, the practices of American Buddhist converts and those of immigrant faithful could not be more different, especially in respect to the visual practices which are the object of our study. Given the history of Buddhist adaptation to indigenous religious traditions, one is not surprised to find immigrants continuing the popular religious practices brought over from their homelands. But this adaptation to cultural contexts suggests that a similar process of adaptation might be happening with native-born Americans attracted to the Buddhist faith. Almost all these converts were raised in some other religious tradition in America (relatively equally divided among Catholic, Protestant, and Jewish traditions—with slightly more Protestants), only three of our sample (of forty) grew up agnostic or atheist. Do these bring with them something of their inherited values and practices? This question naturally suggests itself and will be kept in mind as we listen to the voices from these Buddhist communities.

Given the adaptability of Buddhism and its relatively long history in the United States, the question of the differences between immigrant and native experiences is not a new one. While Buddhism, like Islam, contains a missionary impulse, Buddhist leaders are sometimes wary of the casual acceptance of Buddhist practice in America. (Indeed the larger influence of Buddhism in America, especially in its art and popular culture, is easy to see.) Takeuchi Yoshinori reflects some of these misgivings: "Popular inter-religious culture, in the rush to get to the 'core' of Buddhist truth, is content to plunder a few valuable ideas or practices that can be absorbed easily into other traditions, bypassing the specific character of the transformation Buddhism aims at and the disciplines required to achieve it."[75]

Such worries certainly have not kept large numbers of Americans from seeking religious solace within Buddhism. But how does one under-stand the differences that result between native and immigrant practice? Jan Nattier has proposed that Buddhism practiced in the West has taken on two distinct forms, termed Ethnic and Elite Buddhism.[76] Ethnic Buddhism represents the many varieties of Buddhism practiced by Asian immigrants who retain many popular religious observances; Elite Buddhism is that adopted by (relatively affluent and educated) Americans, mostly pruned of the practices of Asian popular religion. Such a typology is consistent with both the historical character of Buddhism and the radically pluralist reli-gious environment in Los Angeles. Helpful though these are, I will employ these categories sparingly in the discussion that follows, employing more often more descriptive terms, such as converts to Buddhism and immigrant Buddhists, as these are appropriate.[77]

We will be alert, then, for ways in which religious practitioners struggle to adapt (or resist adapting) in their new setting. Obviously this depends in large part on the character and history of the traditions, as we have briefly described these, but it also, necessarily, will reflect something of the American setting as well. Many of our respondents will echo previ-ous studies that have shown that the American setting often encourages deeper religious commitment. Though it may be easier to be a Buddhist in Seoul than in Los Angeles, it might be easier to be a deeply committed Buddhist in Los Angeles than Seoul. As studies at the Center for Religion and Civic Culture at USC in Los Angeles have shown, immigrants can-not help but see the stark contrast between the values of their home tradi-tion and those of American culture at large. These researchers conclude:

---

75. *BS I*, xiv.

76. See Nattier, "Nattier, "Visible and Invisible," 42–49. This is discussed in the con-text of the reception of Zen in the U.S. in *BS II*, 497–510.

77. Respondents and consultants both noted the off-putting nature of the term "elite."

"Hence, [immigrants] find themselves faced with a clear if sometimes painful choice. Those we interviewed often *elected* to embrace their religion more firmly—now making a clear, conscious *choice*—rather than to float along with what they perceived to be the permissive values of American culture."[78] But these considerations taken together serve to raise the major research question of this study: In light of the mix of immigrant and native members in these communities, and considering the cultural context of Southern California, what has changed in these religious traditions? Is there such a thing as a consistently Buddhist, or Muslim, imagination? And if so, in light of our sample, what does this look like? Most importantly, how can these imaginations be understood in relation to each other: how are aesthetic differences and similarities represented and appreciated?

---

78. Miller et al., "Religious Dimensions," 117, emphasis theirs.

Hsi Lai Temple, Whittier, California

Buddhism: Chanting One's Life

Meditation as Spiritual Practice

I am writing these pages on the week before the beginning of Advent, the four weeks leading up to the birthday of Christ in the Christian year. My wife and I have already gone to a service in preparation for Advent. Advent is the beginning of the Christian year, it is a time of putting aside other things and creating a spirit of expectation, of waiting, making ourselves ready for the coming of Christ. Though the season often conspires against this, we want the colors, music, and celebrations of the season to focus our minds on being ready to receive Christ.

Buddhists do not have a season they celebrate like Advent—though they do celebrate Buddha's birthday, but I have the sense that our Buddhist respondents would understand our desire to foster a sense of expectation toward life. Though expressed in a variety of ways, these followers of the Buddhist path wanted to discipline their mind and practice so that it prepares them to receive what they call enlightenment. They also want the images and art they see to help them foster this sense of expectation. Devon was born in Cairo and raised Armenian Orthodox, moving to America in the fourth grade. He converted to Buddhism when he attended a Zen wedding ceremony. He is now a regular attender at the Bodhi Path Sangha in Pasadena. He readily connects his experience of art with spirituality. "When I look at art . . . there is this emotional experience, kind of like joy . . . I realize that the spiritual experience is about feeling joy." This seemed missing from his Christian background, but Buddhism has given him the expectation of experiencing beauty at any moment. He sees his practice cultivating the regular discernment of beauty.

Not surprisingly, meditation in its various forms emerged as the key practice for our Buddhist respondents. Bishop Gengo Akiba, responsible for several hundred Zen temples in the U.S., summed up the Buddhist sense of expectation by noting: "Sitting [meditation] contains the whole of life itself." It is, he says a way to achieve a neutral mind, one that is "not obsessed [by] anything, so it makes our mind healthy. The healthy mind in daily life always can take everything positive[ly]." Meditating is not holding on to ideas, it is a process of releasing them and waiting expectantly.

To Christians this sounds a lot like centering prayer, but when Christians pray they seek to focus their attention on God. When meditating, what do Buddhists focus on? Here the answers given seemed to fall into two different patterns, corresponding to what we might call converts to Buddhism and Buddhists by birth. Patrick, raised in New York State in a Jewish family, converted to Buddhism and meditates at the Buddhist Meditation Center, Against the Stream in Los Angeles (ATS). Visual art never engaged him, he admits: "I like my Buddhism real plain and simple." Meditation for him, he says, is mostly "looking at the back of my eyelids"—ATS being Theravada encourages meditation with one's eyes closed. The point, he says is to be freer and freer from external control, progressively to deconstruct the sense of self and place. What part do visual elements play in this? Patrick knows these are important; in fact he thinks images formed when one's eyes are closed are in many ways stronger. But whether images are internal or external, their strength must be recognized. What has to happen, he believes, is to "learn to work with those [images] skillfully so they bind us less to difficulty . . . We need to work in a very methodical way with what arises in our sight and what arises in our mental imagery that is orienting us all the time." The goal of this is wisdom, the state of being freed from bondage to these external drivers so that life can be lived more compassionately. Seeing images of the Buddha or famous teachers simply encourages Patrick to know that wisdom and compassion are possible; his goal is to embody these. So, Patrick would say one works with images only to eliminate them, because it is "very dangerous for things to earn their worth based on their visual appetitive pleasure."

Tajima is eighty-three years old and has been a widow for twenty-three years. She was born into Buddhism and raised in Kobe, Japan but has lived most of her life in Southern California. She moved there when her husband joined the UCLA medical school faculty. She is a docent at the Getty and the Los Angeles County Museum, and she volunteers regularly at the Zen Soto mission in Little Tokyo. She pointed out that Christians pray to Christ but she prays to her ancestors. At death, Buddhists are given a special name by the priest and their death is celebrated every year—she started coming regularly to Zen Soto Mission when her husband died in 1986. Tajima has set up an altar for her ancestors in her living room, where every morning and evening, she stops to "give a prayer." She prefers to chant in front of her altar in her living room where she sits in the lotus position on her tatami mat, though she also loves to follow the priests' chanting, the drum, and gong at the temple. When asked what images stimulate her meditation, she answers: "I don't think anything, just my routine." Since she grew up with it, it's part of her life, the very familiarity of it has shaped her. But the altar and the chanting seem to provide a clear focus for meditation. These foci seem to be elements Patrick wants to deconstruct.

These two responses represent those who convert and those born Buddhist, or elite and ethnic, that we described in the introduction.[1] Their differences are striking but it would be a mistake to overemphasize them.

---

1. There are those who would argue that Against the Stream represents a somewhat unusual Buddhist case, being so clearly an American punk rock phenomenon. But we found the responses of American born Buddhists in ATS very much like other converts to Buddhism in Bodhi Path and Hsi Lai. This is not to say a more fine-grained study would not uncover significant difference among these groups; our goal is to explore what is common to Buddhist practice generally.

The goal of both is a life that is healthy, free of worry. For Tajima chanting, praying at her altar, hearing the priest's chant in the temple, even her regular volunteering (we all have our gifts that can be used to make the temple a better place, she notes), serve to make her life healthy and peaceful. Patrick's meditation helps him elevate his level of concentration and handle life; it affects everything he does: "The gathered mind," he notes, "is just much more effective." The means may bear different weight and emphasis, something we will reflect on, but the goal of both is the same—what we might call a peaceful life.

Buddhas at Hsi Lai, representing those who have died.

But there is a further similarity that was important to many of our respondents, both native and immigrant. Buddhism is less concerned with believing certain things than with encouraging specific practices that engender the peaceful life. Lama Khedrud the Dharma teacher at Bodhi Path explains: though she teaches about the path, she says, people need to develop their own relationship to meditation. The teaching and the images that are in the space are supportive of the process of meditation but people must pursue this for themselves. Raised as a Protestant Christian she was always troubled by the "gap between where I was and what I believed." The practice of meditation then became very helpful to her—it closed that gap.

The Buddhist tendency to privilege meditation is striking to Christians because Christian practices are emphatically subordinated to the beliefs they signify. Protestant Christians especially are wary of any hint that what we do might "earn" our salvation. What is important about Advent, for example, is not the Advent candles we light or the carols we sing—we do not think these stimulate a spiritual mind; what does this is the reality of God's coming in Christ, on which one reflects during this season. Buddhist faith by contrast places far less emphasis on the ideas behind the practice. Here converts and immigrant Buddhists are of one accord. Patrick insists that Buddhism is a "lived experience," belief is not elaborated; it can only be validated by one's own experience. Arnold, who also meditates at ATS, likens it to Buddhism sacrificing itself. "The more we find we're fixated on the idea of Buddhist, that's just another face of identification and inevitably leads to some suffering . . . and so the practice of Buddhism is becoming less of a Buddhist." This is why he likes the space of ATS, which is white and plain. Its simplicity reminds him that he is not studying Buddhism but himself. Rong, a young monk at Wat Thai, describes what he "learned" in the temple in terms of knowing and not-knowing. The knowing was not about something, which removes you from the present, but about being present in "the rest of your life." So it is better, he summarizes, "to be there in that moment, not thinking of something else."

Miko drives all the way from San Clemente to little Tokyo to volunteer at the Zen Soto Mission. When she bows in the ritual it is an acknowledgment of faith, but in general when she comes to the temple, she says, "we don't think about it all the time . . . it's just part of the life we have . . . It just comes naturally that we do it, you know. Not because we're really thinking about religion." At home she has an altar where she honors those who have died. She admits that she rarely meditates, but her volunteering, hearing the chanting, seeing the statues of Buddha, she thinks, "gives you peace of mind."

To a Christian outsider, Buddhist attitudes toward belief seem curious—they are, as Patrick says, "thin." But Buddhists see the elimination of belief as a clear asset. In fact some of our respondents who converted from Christianity left that faith over difficulties with the "what and why" of belief. We have already heard Lama Khedrud's sense of the gap between her belief and her practice. Kim, who mediates at Hsi Lai Temple, grew up as an evangelical Christian, but he says: "I didn't like the answers I was getting." In 2001 he went to hear the Dalai Lama and "That was the day I knew I was supposed to be a Buddhist." He says that when he comes to the quiet of the Hsi Lai temple space, "It feels as though a weight is lifted off my shoulders." Melanie was raised in the Foursquare Pentecostal denomination, but when she found out her church believed her Catholic friends would go to hell, she felt she had to leave. Others found the Christian emphasis on believing simply strange. Gabriel was born and raised in California of Thai parents. When we interviewed him he was twenty-three and had been living as a monk for three months at Wat Thai Temple (in Thai Buddhism, practitioners are encouraged to spend some time as a monk in a temple or monastery; it is not necessarily a lifelong calling as in Christianity). He claims he "tried out" other religions, presumably Christianity among them. He says of these experiences: "They tried to make me believe, but I couldn't believe, so I had to tell them 'sorry, I can't do this.'" He refers to his time in the temple, which, he says, he is doing for his grandmother and for himself, as "nice and peaceful. It's quiet, and it's keeping me out of trouble." (He confessed he likes to dance and this "got him into a lot of trouble"). Being in the temple then was a time to hone his spiritual life. The other monks encourage him to pray at night "to clean up his mind." He likes the peace and quiet in the temple. He says: "I don't have to worry about the real world because . . . I'm here for myself, and [when] I'm finished, I would want to feel like a new man. Because like right now, I feel like I should cleanse my body, clean it up, like kind of get rid of all the bad things that I have done and start afresh."

Sato provides a particularly striking example of the diminished role of belief and the relief she felt letting go of this. She was raised in Mexico in a conservative Baptist family. Her beloved father was a pastor who diligently taught his children and refused to allow them baptism until he was absolutely certain they understood what they were doing. And he tried his best to answer the many questions that Sato had. But he died when she was still young and was no longer around to answer her questions. Some time later she visited the Zen Soto mission and found a peace that she hadn't found elsewhere. Though initially bothered by the images, she relates: "The sitting is what kept me anchored and in balance . . . I felt it was being very healing." Still she was troubled, "I had a million questions," she reports. But one day a monk approached her and said simply: "There are no answers." From that day, she says, the questions went away. And she eventually was ordained (and given a Japanese name). She loves the peace of sitting where "you don't do anything. That's it. You just sit and breathe. But it changes [your] life."

For these, the experience of peace and serenity stand in contrast with the need to believe certain things. It would be wrong, however, to imply teaching has no part in the process. Rong, the young monk we interviewed, was in his third year in the Wat Thai Temple. He likes learning about the

Sanskrit chants (he allows that earlier the chants had made him calm even though he didn't know what they meant), and the different kinds of meditation, which he described to us as enstatic and ecstatic—suggesting depth and breadth. He understands now that the chants contain particular teachings about Buddhism. Interestingly, it seems the primarily elite temples, ATS and Bodhi Path, place a greater emphasis on the teaching in connection with their programs. Respondents consistently say they enjoy what they call "sitting" with their teacher. But, even there, the emphasis is clearly on the meditation practices that are described and facilitated by the instruction.

To be sure, the content of teaching was not ignored altogether, especially by the monks at Hsi Lai, or by Bishop Akiba, or Lama Khedrub of Bodhi Path. But even for these leaders teaching played a suggestive rather than a defining role. Venerable Miao Hsi, a monk at Hsi Lai, in her interview explained that the Buddha nature resides in all people. Bishop Akiba described the importance of the life of Buddhist monks and teachers: "Through . . . daily life we transmit our teaching," not only through our teaching. Lama Khedrub grew up in Encino, California as an active Protestant and still has positive feelings about her past. But her religious experience left her with the sense that she was missing something. There was a gap, as we have seen, between where she was and what she believed. She was impressed with Buddhists she met who seemed to "take responsibility for their own emotions." She began to meditate and found it helpful; it did away with her feelings of discomfort. In her training to be a Lama in Boulder, Colorado she was exposed to Buddhist imagery and she came to understand how this relates to the practice of meditation. She described for us the many-armed image (Chenresig), for example, which embodies the all-seeing and all-embracing character of Buddhism. It stands ready, she pointed out, to go into action—not to turn away from suffering but to move toward it. But when you look at this, she says, you should "take it into your heart . . . So when you visualize that, that's some quality that you're relating to . . . as being qualities that you have to . . . learn how to . . . own [and] realize." This is the purpose of art, she thinks, even as it is the purpose of her teaching.

The four-armed Chenresig, outside the Wat Thai Temple,
represents the all-seeing and embracing nature.

So the content of teaching, as of practices and images, finds its goal in producing particular qualities that characterize a peaceful life. Interestingly Lama Khedrub has an altar in her home, a shrine with flowers and candles. Though it does not honor ancestors in the way immigrant practice does, she says it beckons her. It says: "Come over here, here's a little rest from the rest of your life." Belief has moved to the background, or perhaps it has become tacit rather than explicit. In struggling to describe his time in the temple, Gabriel, the young monk at Wat Thai, might help us grasp this Buddhist way of knowing. He describes what he is doing in the temple as seeking a fresh start. Better yet, he says, it is like trying to bring things into focus. Sometimes life is like "one of those media players," he thinks, "where it just like goes in and out . . . It's a little wavy out there [in the world] . . . I start to understand but then I drop back down . . . I'd like to make the wave not so big but smaller . . . because like right now . . . It's all a blur." Meditation is part of the work of bringing things into focus. This is what matters to Gabriel: "I'm just trying to figure out what works and what doesn't work."

Though it seems images do not play as central a role in Buddhism as they do, say, in Catholicism or Orthodoxy, I was struck by how often descriptions of the goal are framed in visual or aesthetic terms: one seeks focus, enlightenment, feelings of peace and joy. And in the popular imagination, Buddha images would appear to be central to the faith. What role then do Buddhist images, and the art of the tradition, play in the practice? How do they express meaning?

Buddhist Images and Symbols: Bringing Life into Focus

It may seem strange to call Buddhism an "aniconic" faith; when outsiders think of Buddhism, the first thing that comes to mind is likely to be the sitting Buddha holding his hands in his lap. But, as we have noted in the introduction, in its early history Buddhism avoided making any image of the Buddha. And throughout its history the covenant that it has made with images has been complex; images are often prominent, but their role is fraught. Our respondents agree that art and the process of visualization are important but when pressed to say what role they play in meditation they hesitate. On the one hand, as Jeu Wei Shi one of the monks at Hsi Lai says, Buddhism encourages symbolism. Everything we do and wear is symbolic, she points out. Monks shave their heads to emphasize the search for inner beauty; they wear clothes the color of the earth to emphasize their oneness with the earth. As she says, this symbolism "is really pervasive in our life. When we say Buddhism is a way of life, we really mean it." On the other hand external symbols are inherently limited in their power. As another monk at Hsi Lai explains, one studies such symbolism as a special subject, but it is not central, she says, "It's not the teaching." Rong, who is spending time as a monk at Wat Thai in the course of his interview, attempted to explain this tension. He is the twenty-three-year-old monk who earlier described the things he was learning at the temple about chanting, meditating, and the proper forms of breathing. When asked about whether the images connect with his religious experience, he said they did not. He acknowledged there were many symbols in Buddhism that you can study and understand. There is meaning to them that you can understand, but he points out, "you cannot understand that within yourself. If you cannot understand everything that is within yourself then it is worthless to imagine it. Imagine that it is something that makes you better." This process, as he pointed out earlier, is not about knowing. Indeed you must "accept that you [do] not know anything at all." Little by little the process of meditating leads you deeper into yourself; in the final analysis, he thinks, symbols are no help here.

Still on one level images symbolize or stand for qualities that one wants to embody, as we have seen. Devon, who came to America from Egypt in fourth grade, experiences beauty as a joy that he connects with spirituality. He insists "visualization is an important part of Buddhist practice." The image of the Buddha represents for him the enlightened quality within himself. Edna, who was raised a Catholic and also comes to Bodhi Path, likes the positive and peaceful role these play in her practice. At Bodhi Path where Devon and Edna meditate, Lama Khedrub will occasionally use guided meditation. Edna describes how the Lama will use imagery when the class is fidgeting around. "She kind of throws in some guided meditation, like 'imagine Buddha right above you, in white light, melting into your top crown of your head, and become like him, and become him.' It kind of helps [keep] your mind from wandering. So, becoming—it's almost like becoming one with the image." Interestingly the idea of becoming one with the image didn't seem to fit with her experience of Catholic imagery. How does one become one with the cross, she wondered? "I didn't want to connect with pain. I thought there might have been something better to emphasize in religion . . . I know that they say that he died for us. Yes, but you don't [need to] make us feel guilty about it [she laughed]." In her Buddhist practice, by contrast, the images are "calm and collected." This helps tremendously, she thinks: "If we look at the images . . . then that gives us an image for ourselves to become like that: calm and collected."

This points to a second positive role that images can play. Beyond standing for qualities, they can also become emotional triggers that motivate one to pursue the Buddhist path. Images, Buddhists believe, do things for people. Arnold meditates at Against the Stream (ATS). His earliest memories are of religious art; though raised Jewish he finds images of Mother Mary "intriguing and mystically beautiful." But now it is images of the three jewels (the Buddha, the Dharma, and the Sangha) that move him most deeply. "Whenever I see a portrayal of the three jewels my heart feels light. I really love that [sic] image: The image of the sitting Buddha in meditation is very powerful . . . for me." These images serve as little "post-it signs" that bring joy and encouragement to him. He took a pilgrimage to India a few years ago and sat under the Bodhi tree, where the Buddha received his enlightenment. Some leaves fell while he meditated there and he brought them home and hung them framed on his wall. When he looks at them, he says, "my mind goes straight to the ideal of bliss and enlightenment." He is emotionally touched by these images; they not only stand for qualities but, he believes, they actually move him toward the condition of enlightenment.

So images can stand for qualities of the enlightened life and they can function as motivation to pursue this life, but at a certain point one has to go beyond the external image. Several respondents referred to them as something beginning students may need but more advanced meditators do not. As Rong put this, one has to understand them "within oneself." In this respect images can be dangerous, they can distract one from the path. Patrick who meditates and teaches at ATS admits that images can be signs that wisdom and compassion are possible—this plays a certain role in assuring one of the line of people trying to "wake up." But he says, "as far [as] actual meditative practice, at that point all kind of conscious efforts to generate imagery is released." He thinks the Christian tradition has often used imagery not as an instrument of legitimacy, as he put it, but as "legitimacy itself." He worries that building ideas of self from images can devolve "into ritualistic devotional practice" that distracts from the freedom of the lived experience.[2]

Patricia of Bodhi Path, who has studied dance anthropology, describes this deeper role of images in terms of her earlier experience with Theravada Buddhism (she is one of several among our respondents who had experience in more than one Buddhist tradition). There the focus was on meditation and breathing, which includes both having the sensation of breath but also visualizing breath. In this way the "mind can create a visual and somatic, or a visual and auditory experience through suggestion, even though it doesn't make a product." Now having come to Bodhi Path, which is in the Tibetan (and Mahayana) tradition of Buddhism, she has started to "use" the Buddha. Lama Khedrud is very specific about how one appropriates the image, Patricia notes. "You sort of compress the image—you never take it to be the person—you compress the image and you incorporate it into your own heart. So, it becomes your essence, your being. It becomes . . . ultimateness, absoluteness. And that's in you." Visualization is only a tool, she insists, to create these kinds of experiences (she thinks this is true of all religious traditions). The image of Buddha comes to "gather all the things that you understand about spiritual truth, and aspire to. Then, to incorporate that, like eating the body of Christ, is to help you become that."

2. When hearing Patrick's story one wonders how much of his wariness about images stems from his secular Jewish background. He admits that for him the ritual of the synagogue was always empty. "As far as an actual theological framework that we subscribe[d] to, it was always empty." The idea of God was "beside the point."

It is interesting that Patricia, raised an agnostic Jew, can reference eucharistic imagery as an example of the collecting and gathering of meaning represented by the Buddha.

But is this compressing of imagery in fact something that characterizes all religious traditions? The Christian may be tempted to respond that Christian worshipers actually do eat the symbol of Christ; they do not take it into themselves as an aspect of meditation. There is clearly overlap here, and I struggle to understand how these practices are the same and how they may be different. But one way of describing the difference might be as follows: For Patricia the image and its meaning—which for many respondents is indistinguishable, is assimilated into the practice of meditation, that is into the discipline of freeing one's mind. For the Christian the image of Christ in the Eucharist is a site of contemplation, I meditate on the way Christ's death and resurrection becomes spiritual nourishment in the Eucharist. I think the distinction between "practice" and "contemplation" might get at what seems to me an important difference. In Buddhist practice, meaning is submerged in the physical and mental practice. To rephrase a term from medieval theology: for Buddhists, truth is in order to discipline the practice. For Christians the practice of the Eucharist is submerged into the larger project of being incorporated into Christ's life—truth is in order to godliness. But the challenge my Buddhist friends raise for me is the following: the practice of meditation for Buddhists has the real-world component of making one more compassionate. What real-world practices does my project, what I am calling contemplation, call for?

In fact Christian imagery came up quite frequently in the interviews—something that is not surprising given the dominant presence of Christian symbols in the culture. I will comment on this below, but there is one further use of imagery that strikes me as unique and important to Buddhism. The Buddha is not only a typical Buddhist image but suggests a type of representation that is important to Buddhists. The image of Buddha represents in visual form one who has devoted himself to the way of enlightenment. In this way the Buddha is a living image of the path, he embodies his teaching. Betty who meditates at ATS was born and raised in New York City and was dedicated to Mary by her Catholic mother. As she drifted away from Catholicism and sought to live a peaceful life, she discovered that she was really living in a Buddhist way. Images in the temples kind of support that way, she says, but they play no role in her meditation. Yet later she confesses that she can look at the Buddha and say: "It worked for him, it would work for me." The image represents a model she can follow.

Buddha image at the Hsi Lai Temple.

Several respondents referred to images, whether of the Buddha or of their real life teachers, that have become living models of the path for them. Venerable Jue Wei Shi at Hsi Lai keeps a picture of the Buddha and of her teacher in her small room: "It's a form of respect that I have the pictures . . . my master cannot be with me all the time and I can't be with him all the time, so having a picture of my master up reminds me of his teachings." She goes on to review some of his humanistic teachings. The picture reminds her of all that. The Buddha image is a reminder as well but also a stimulus to repent: "The Buddha statue gives me the opportunity to repent before the Buddha, to ask for help and not to think of myself as being the egoistic super powerful, omnipotent person that I would like to think I am." For Val the first thing she thinks about when reflecting on her experience at

ATS is the teacher Noah Levine sitting in front on a dais in front of a large wall with Thai Buddhas. She likes the idea of the sangha gathered around the Dharma-teaching represented by Noah—not that they are focusing on Noah as a deity, but they are focused on the teaching that he represents. April also grew up Roman Catholic and comes to meditate at ATS, as she says to "sit with Noah." Growing up as a Catholic in a Mexican family in L.A., imagery was important to her. But that imagery she now finds violent and distracting and prefers the stripped down feel of ATS. She has sat with Noah, and the other teachers there, for years now and the small sangha allows her to have a personal relationship with Noah and with the teachings.

"Sitting" in meditation with Noah Levine, Against The Stream Sangha.

Patrick, as we have seen, likes his Buddhism plain and simple, but he does appreciate photos of the great Dharma teachers. In their very faces he thinks he can discern the path they have taken. He says of these pictures: "People begin to take on a certain look as they get freer and freer and that's evident in the photograph[s]." Their self-consciousness is gone, he thinks. For these, images of teachers can do more than simply remind them of the teaching, they come to represent that truth in visual form. The images take on the aura of the teaching they represent, and they become living images for their followers. But the process these followers use is the same as with images more generally, first the quality is embodied in the representation, then in the course of meditation it is to be internalized in the person who practices.

Images of teachers and religious leaders have traditionally played a significant role in Buddhist rituals, serving as a kind of icon. Griffith Foulk and Robert Sharf have described their role in the medieval Zen (Chan) tradition: "The portrait of the abbot, like the living abbot on his high seat, is thus properly viewed as a religious icon—it is a manifestation of Buddhahood and a focus for ritual worship. As such, the portrait is functionally equivalent to the mummified remains of the abbot, to the relics of the Buddha, or to a *stupa*, in that it denotes the Buddha's presence in his very absence."[3]

This ritual use of images is especially interesting in the Zen tradition, which is usually seen as the most iconoclastic of the Buddhist traditions. But these scholars have shown that use of iconic images, which originated in the Zen monasteries, was widespread in medieval Buddhism, and represents a long-standing precedent of practices followed today. But note, according to Foulk and Sharf, the images communicate the central truth of *anatta*, or non-self, in both affirming and effacing the presence of Buddha. In other words the image is meant to be "worked with skillfully," as Patrick put it, so that they convey the non-permanence meditation emphasizes.

The ritual use of icons in Buddhism recalls the icons in the Eastern Orthodox tradition, where images of Christ, Mary, or the saints are seen to communicate the reality of the heavenly order to those who pray before them. Though this deserves much more study than we are able to give it here, it would seem the reference of these images, and thus their ritual use, carry very different meanings. There are similarities of course. Both traditions believe the images reflect the qualities that these figures represent. But their very different metaphysical commitments issue in opposing attitudes toward the images themselves. The Buddhist seeks in a sense to deconstruct the image, the Orthodox believer wants to affirm the image and its heavenly location, and to indwell the reality pictured more fully.

Ritual Practices

From time to time we have made reference to ritual acts in our discussion of images, and these deserve further discussion in their own right. Many

---

3. Quoted in Lopez Jr., *Critical Terms for the Study of Buddhism*, 47.

of the immigrant Buddhists mentioned the altars mounted as memorials to ancestors that they have in their homes. Rev. Kojima of Zen Soto Mission notes that immigrant Buddhists do not always have altars in their homes, though a death in the family is likely to motivate them to put one up. These places become part of the extended family, they make present the absent member(s) of the family. Tajima tells us she offers prayer to them each day. Mako of Zen Soto Mission, when she passes by, gives a little "thank you to my parents, my sister . . . [telling them] you should help us have a better life as long as we are living . . . let's have a nice day today. Let's not make it too hard." Two of the women respondents kept a little Japanese pastry that our researcher brought as a thank you, so that they could take it home for their husbands—both of whom had passed away. But though they admit they don't think much about these practices—these are just part of the life they have grown up with—they would all say the altars play a role in ordering their life and making it more peaceful.

On Buddha's birthday there is a celebration at Hsi Lai Temple that includes spreading fresh flowers over the large pool of water. Four smaller Buddhas stand around the pool and there is provision at each for people to wash the image of Buddha. Alongside these are boxes for donations and tables with Buddhist literature on it. Young and old take part in this ritual cleansing, scooping the water and pouring it over the Buddha—signifying

Washing the Buddha on Buddha's birthday at Hsi Lai Temple.

the cleansing of their own Buddha nature. On a table at the Bodhi Path in Pasadena there may be an offering of fruit or water. Devon from an Egyptian-Armenian family likes the symbolism of these simple offerings. The water, he notes, is put in bowls all the way to the top "and when you discard the water you don't just throw it away . . . you pour it on a plant" or give it to someone to drink. It becomes a gift that expresses the generosity that one seeks in the path.

Though these simple rituals were general across the communities we studied, there is some disagreement over what practices are necessary and the role they should play. As might be expected, the converts to Buddhism tend to de-emphasize such ritual. In fact Noah Levine founded ATS in part to get back to what he calls the core of Buddhism, to strip away the accumulation of rituals associated with various cultures. As Norman, a regular ATS attender, describes this intention: "The humble intention that ATS is founded on is let's go back to what Buddha said. Let's go back to the core. Let's not do these rituals, whether they be Japanese, Thai, Tibetan. So many of these rituals are so tied into whatever culture they belong to . . . So I appreciate the letting go of some of the baggage and so the teaching then for me becomes a lot more accessible and applicable." He says that he wouldn't keep coming back if the teachings did not apply to his life as a twentysomething Westerner who likes to chase girls, if it did not give him practical ways to apply the Dharma to his everyday life. There is some irony here. ATS may have tried to get back to the core teachings of Buddhism, but it grew out of a particular San Francisco punk culture and so represents, in its own way, a contemporary example of the cultural adaptability of Buddhism. Still Norman's testimony is significant. I am struck by how easily these same views could be expressed by a recent convert to an evangelical form of Protestantism, who was relieved to leave the rituals and symbols of, say, his Catholic background. Both seek a faith that works in their everyday life, one that gets them back to the core and essence of a spiritual experience.

But the pull of Buddhism can work in the other direction as well. Kim, a convert from evangelicalism at Hsi Lai, responds to the draw of traditional practices. He is very articulate about the Christian use of art in the crucifix as a reminder of the teaching that Christ died for our sins and opened up the way to eternal life. But he is drawn to the simplicity of the Buddha sitting calmly with his palm open and the other hand touching ground, this is "a huge help for me. It's in my eyes, it's a way of remembering to see the Buddhist path any way you look." And he has incorporated this experience with the image into his regular ritual. When he comes to the temple he will walk up the steps, slowly, to ground himself, enter the hall, and make three prostrations. He says: "I work to check [my] ego at the door. Bowing is really good for that," he thinks. But he is quick to say that this is not bowing to the Buddha statue, "you're bowing to remember . . . to work toward lack of ego." He finds it peaceful to sit in the main shrine for a minute and make more prostrations before he leaves. This ritual practice provides a structure and orientation that his Christian past did not.

Both Devon and Kim represent one consistent characteristic of elite Buddhists: They were anxious to explain to us, often in detail, the path they have chosen and the reasons for their choice. They would not resonate with the frequent refrain of ethnic Buddhists who insist "I don't think about it" or "it's automatic for me" or "part of the life we have." There is a further irony here as well. Buddhism in general represents a practice, a path, rather than a set of beliefs; the weight of emphasis is on the practice not the beliefs, which, as Patrick put it, are rather thin. Still these converts are typically articulate in describing this thinness, they are careful to explain why these particular practices matter. Perhaps this is a function of the sample that we interviewed, perhaps it is reflection of the relatively high level of education, but it is consistent enough to call for further reflection—something we will want to return to in the conclusion.

Buddhist and Christian Imagery

As Christian observers we were naturally intrigued to see that these Buddhist respondents had a great deal to say about Christian imagery, either from their own past experience or from what they observed in the Christian culture surrounding them. Some of these memories surely resulted, as we have said, from the dominance of Christian imagery in American culture. Val who is part of the community at ATS did not grow up with a religious background. She likes the imagery associated with Buddhism and finds it comforting. But when asked what images have stuck with her she mentions the Virgin Mary, perhaps, she thinks, because she lost her mother when she was young. She finds the image comforting: "I've been drawn to that image incredibly even though I'm not a Christian." Norman, we have seen, though raised Jewish also found the image of Mother Mary, "intriguing and mystically beautiful." This image helped him frame his understanding of spirituality and beauty.

But it was those raised with Christian imagery who most struggled over the role of imagery in their new faith. The forming of the Buddhist mind always takes place in relation to the spaces and visual practices people bring with them, and this was especially true of those raised in strong Christian visual environments. Pablo was born in Lima, Peru and raised a Catholic but was not practicing his faith when he became an adult—he had come to resent organized religion. He was drawn to the Bodhi Path group through his encounter with the Tibetan struggle for independence and his exposure to the Dalai Lama. He sensed a connection there, and yet his background made him fearful. He felt the "whole structure of the meaning of life that I had grow[n] up with" was being challenged. Do I really want to go there, he wondered? One day he saw a postcard at the sangha that said: "Happiness of others is more important than our own happiness." This was the deciding factor: what could possibly be wrong with that? How could he go to hell for believing this? He decided then and there that this was the path for him. "OK, now I'm in it," he said to himself. "It was just opened up for me . . . [it was] revolutionary."

What about all the images from his Catholic past? How did they impact him? He readily recalls the rosaries, the crosses, an image of St. Martin, but growing up they had no influence on him. His feeling about this visual past is especially interesting. He says, in words that echoed our immigrant Buddhist respondents, "I thought it just part of life, part of the routine, part of everyday. It was just there. It was just there." It was there and he thought it had no power over him, until he began to move away from it. But now, he says, "I have an altar, a shrine, a shrine room. And I have an image . . . of the Buddha. I have some images of deities which . . . seem like beings, but they're really . . . just an aspect of our mind." They represent the compassion he seeks to embody. Having chosen the Buddhist path, its images have come alive for him. But they come to life not simply while looking at them, but in the practices: "As you do these practices, there's a blessing, there is something going on. You're turning something . . . working the soil."

At the end of the interview we asked Pablo what he makes now of the images from his Catholic past? Does he think about them at all? Yes, he admitted, sometimes he does and smiles when he thinks about his shrine: maybe, he thinks, he's come back to his childhood. But now, he says, "I understand it differently. And I even understand [that] Buddhism . . . really gave me understanding of my own religious background, understanding of saints and images and these saints that we use as humans." Though now he uses these differently, as inspiration for what he is doing, as part of the practice: "I have to surrender," he says. For Pablo at least part of the covenant that he is forming with images as a Buddhist includes a reworking of the visual experiences of the past—this is part of the soil in which he digs.

Ramona visits Bodhi Path regularly. She grew up in Soviet Armenia, and came to the U.S. when she started college. She still goes to the Armenian church, for special events, but she says "it doesn't appeal to me at all. I just do it because it is part of my culture." Still, she carries with her the visual experiences of sitting in Armenian churches and visiting monasteries while growing up. This represents what is impressive to her: "Whatever appeals to the senses, not the mind." In this respect the plain environment of Bodhi Path and the makeshift altar does not appeal to her, "it seems kind of fake to me." But she connects with the people and she is attracted by the offerings of fruit, flowers, and the incense. And the practice of meditation helps her "clear her head." But when asked what image has made the deepest impression on her, she answers: "When I was a child growing up . . . on one of the walls of my mother's bedroom there was a picture of the Virgin Mary with the child. And that is still very much a sacred picture that I would hold in my head and my heart." This, not the Buddha, is her favorite sacred picture. But it is now incorporated into a new set of practices. In fact one might say, the image has been reframed by these new arrangements. What does this image mean to her now? "Just the whole idea of motherhood and embodiment of kindness and the caring and devotion—everything that I feel, I would say is embodied in [that] wall picture." Certainly, Christians would agree that Mary embodies these qualities, but this is not the primary role that Mary plays. For Christians, Mary plays a particular role within a specific narrative and accompanying practices. But for Ramona that narrative and those practices have lost their meaning. Mary still carries emotional weight, but this has been recontextualized into her Buddhist faith. One might even say that Ramona has made Mary into a Buddhist image.

Mary, a regular visitor to Hsi Lai Temple, has done something similar with the image of Jesus. Mary was raised in small town near Reno, Nevada in a nominally Methodist family. She remembers especially a picture of Jesus where her mother used to hide their money (her father had died when she was four). It is connected in her mind with a vivid encounter she had with Jesus when she was young. As a small child she contracted rheumatic fever, developed a hole in her heart, and missed a year of school. Her illness forced them to move in with her grandmother. One night when she was alone with her sister she had a dream that she had died, and in this dream she was backing away from light into darkness when she bumped into someone who turned out to be Jesus. At the same time her dad was there in front of her, telling her to take his hand and go with him. But Jesus said to her: "I want you to go back . . . don't take his hand, you are not going to die—you have a long time to live, go back." She woke up screaming and told her sister that Jesus had saved her. A few years ago she started coming to this Buddhist temple, but she carries with her this strong connection to Jesus. She has found the temple to be a place where she experiences a peace that she had not found in her previous religious experience, but she has not given up her connection to this past. "You can feel the peacefulness and the compassion and the love, but you are not getting it from the Buddha statues, because it's inside you." She feels the peace and compassion in the space and in the people when she is here. She especially was struck by the experience of washing the Buddha on his birthday: "I was washing one of the Buddhas and I could almost feel the energy coming off of it . . . It was just such an honor to wash that Buddha." She has even taken a Buddha to her workplace where she works with troubled children. The hardest thing she does, she admits, is show compassion in her everyday life—she acknowledges she is a long way from enlightenment.

These images and rituals have come to shape Mary's life in a distinctly Buddhist way, though the image of Jesus continues to play an important role in this process. On that day when she was a child, Mary says, "I really do believe I touched Jesus' robe." Afterward when she was tested in San Francisco, the hole in her heart had healed. When she dies she is sure that her mother will be there, and Jesus will be there too, though, she laughs, "don't tell that to the Buddha here!" In the end, however, she finds no difficulty in reconciling the images of Jesus and Buddha. Buddhism in her mind allows one also to believe in Jesus. In fact she thinks that Jesus and Buddha are the same—both loving and compassionate figures. The energy of Buddha is in everyone, and she says, "I guess Jesus is in everybody too." And Mary believes Jesus is part of the process of birth, death, and rebirth that she has come to accept with her Buddhist sensibilities. Jesus still occupies an important place in her life, but the constellation in which she lives and moves, is clearly Buddhist.

Space and the Role of the Temple

While it was generally agreed that one can meditate anywhere—indeed, as we will note, the goal of Buddhist practice is to increase the scope of mindfulness until it covers the whole of life, the place where the sangha gathers was very important for many of our respondents. One question we asked concerned the role space played in their meditation, a question that was intentionally open ended to allow for a variety of (literál and metaphoric) interpretations of place and space. And other questions asked about the visual elements that one sees in their temple or meeting room. Mei, a seventy-year-old woman who came to the U.S. from Taiwan in 1979, loves coming to Hsi Lai Temple. She sees it as a place of peace. "You feel very peaceful . . . because of the spaciousness and . . . the energy there." This sense of peace, she says, is enhanced by smells and sounds: incense, the morning bell, and the evening gong. "Every time you hear that, it's some

The bell at Hsi Lai Temple.

thing awakening within you." But in the end she thinks it's the people, the monastics (monks), and those who meditate who define the space. "When you get a group of people there with the same intention—to find peace—I think it will be more peaceful there. It's not only the shrine." This testimony was repeated numerous times—the place of meditation is a peaceful place, sacred in a way, a place to feel at home, just as worshipers from many traditions would speak about their space. (In fact Mei thinks one can find this peaceful space in a church or a mosque.)

But is there something unique to Buddhist spaces? Much like images, in Buddhism space is not meant to call attention to itself, but to encourage self-examination and meditation. And several respondents did mention the role of space in their meditation. April at ATS feels space is important in that the whole purpose is to create a space for letting things go. This "letting go" should have its physical counterpart in the place of meditation, she thinks. "The way that we arrange our cushions is to have enough room so we're comfortable but still intimate, so it doesn't feel like we're in a huge [place] . . . far apart from each other where we can't communicate." The best space is one where one is free to move, not feeling constrained, yet very close and warm at the same time. Arnold, who is part of the same sangha, likes the blank walls, and the intimacy, which allows the space to become sacred for him. Like the image of Buddha it speaks of peace and comfort. Rachel likes the space at ATS because it is clean and simple, "there's not a feeling of clutter . . . It has a good feeling." Though in a very different setting and with a vastly different background, Mahasi, who came to the U.S. from Thailand when she was nineteen, can say similar things about the space of her Wat Thai Temple: "I like to listen to the monks when they chant . . . you can follow the chanting with them and then it makes you concentrate and you let go of everything . . . It keeps you calm, at peace. And I like to hear the sounds . . . And the monks, they cannot touch the female, so you feel, I feel safe here and I can do things . . . help out."

Melanie feels the energy when she visits the Hsi Lai Temple, and the "wisdoms of the past, present and future." She connects this with all the images and statues that are there but also with the people that are there, the collective oneness they share evokes a sense of peace. As Kim puts it, everywhere you look when you walk into the shrine you see the Buddha, it reminds you of the path you've chosen. When I am there, he says, "it feels . . . as though a weight has been lifted off my shoulders." The temple space seems to attract practitioners for many reasons, but for all it is an arena that becomes charged as they engage in the various forms of meditation. Devon who helps put up the altar at Bodhi Path notes the act of putting these things there "shifts the quality of the place . . . into a sacred space." When Pablo comes into Bodhi Path he tries to get in tune with the space. "This is where it is happening," he notes; the point is to tune in to the space. As with the images, the space is incorporated into the practices of meditation, one might say it is put into play by these. The practices give the space meaning and make it come alive.

One of the commonest misperceptions that outsiders have about Buddhism is that it merely encourages an individual and private practice—each person does their own meditation and pursues a solitary path. Meditation is indeed a personal and private practice, but for many of our respondents it also has a corporate dimension. The sangha as we saw in the introduction is one of the three jewels of Buddhism and while this means strictly those who devote themselves to the Buddhist way—often by withdrawing into monasteries, in general it has come to mean those who gather together with the monks and lamas to meditate. Venerable Jue Wei Shi says of Hsi Lai Temple: "The main shrine itself is a place for many of us to gather in a sacred space, to gather in communion, and give one another strength as well as remind ourselves of the sacred." Indeed when she is asked what she likes best about the space of Hsi Lai, she says, it is the people. In fact she thinks "it's the people who make the images come alive." Without the people the images would not be "clean," she thinks. In different ways respondents reiterated these ideas. At Bodhi Path many like that, before they settle in to meditate, they take time to connect with one another, getting caught up on their lives. And in fact this "getting caught up" becomes a part of the practice. Dan who was raised as a Congregational Protestant, studied a lot and meditated on his own before he came to ATS. He realized the sangha is there to support him and put him in the right place. The room itself does not do that for him, but the people do. The best thing about coming to Bodhi Path, Edna thinks, is the community. "The feeling that it gives you spiritually. The support." Ramona in fact feels much closer to the people, than the pictures that are there in Bodhi Path. "They (the pictures) do not do it for me," she says. But she enjoys the connection with people who come. Similarly, Val says of her comrades at ATS: "I love my friends, the sangha members. I feel very loved and love them. Some people I don't know but I feel glad that they're there and they're part of something. It's very powerful to meditate with people. I mean I can meditate at home, but there's something great about sitting in a room with fifty to one hundred people and just settling in. It's quiet but you know that you're all there to-gether." She loves the night she joins her friends. It is her sacred night, her church.

Members of Against the Stream converse before meditating.

For the temples with ethnic traditions, the sense of community is reinforced by the practices of enjoying food together, and bringing one's children to learn the language and culture. Jihn is in his twenties. He was born and raised in L.A,, though his parents were born in Thailand. He has started a Buddhist club at his school and especially enjoys coming to the Wat Thai Temple. He comes to see his friends, have some good food—it is, he says, a place of good memories. So the practices of Buddhism are personal, but they are in an important sense carriers of a rich history. One learns from the teacher an aspect and stream of the tradition and joins in with those who over time have traveled in the Buddhist way. None felt any tension between the personal and the corporate, but the distinction raises a related question: how does this highly personal practice translate into life in the broader world?

Buddhism and Everyday Life

One might imagine that there would be a tension in Buddhist attempts to apply meditation to their everyday lives. Frequently respondents told of their attempts to be more compassionate or better. But compassion is exercised in the realm of samsara or illusion, while the goal of Buddhist practice—enlightenment, in a fundamental sense, is release from this world of illusion. How do they reconcile this tension? As I reflect on this, however, I can see that there is a similar tension in Christianity. For the Christian the tension is expressed in terms of the transcendent goal of life—communion with God and the necessity of living this out here and now (which in some Christian traditions is destined, as in Buddhism, to pass away). It will be instructive for Christians then to see how Buddhists work with this tension.

The traditional teaching of Buddhist practice is sometimes called the "middle path." Venerable Jue Wei Shi described this in her interview. We know that there are many people who don't have enough to eat. This does not mean that when we come to a buffet we refuse to eat, but it also does not mean that we stuff ourselves until we are too full. This discernment is the middle path. She says: "Middle path means looking at the conditions of myself and others, what is right. So, having that understanding . . . then [this] helps us in making decision[s] in our lives that [are] compassionate, wise, brave." In fact, she says, all the external practices and images are to be internalized, so they "become part of my mental imagery." This helps purify her consciousness of what should be desired and what should not.

We saw in the introduction that the first step of the ancient "Path to Purification" encompassed the ethical prescriptions based on the precepts of Buddhism, which, in the second step, are to be taken to heart in the processes of meditation so that, thirdly, enlightenment becomes possible. What was interesting was that different respondents tended to focus on either the first or second of these steps in thinking about their everyday life. Venerable Shi was clearly seeking to present these as a unified practice, as it is in normative Buddhism. But in general the immigrant Buddhist response tended to focus on the precepts, while the converts stressed the processes and effects of meditation. Consider the testimony of Sunthorn, who came to the U.S. from Thailand in 1976 and is seventy-two years old. She has a large Buddha in her home and prays morning and evening in front of it—though she says she only meditates once a week. When pressed to say how the Buddha strengthens her, she responded: "When you're nice to the people, most people [will be] nice to you." Don't steal, take a life, or trust in possessions—these things are "not nice." Others, all ethnic Buddhists, mentioned these "five rules" as basic to Buddhist practice.

For many of these, coming to volunteer at the temple has become part of their everyday life. Miko is frequently to be found at the Zen Soto

Mission, even though she has to commute sixty miles from San Clemente. She enjoys helping out there but she doesn't think about it as religious, "it's part of the life we have." In fact she admits that she doesn't meditate, either at the temple or at home. "That's for serious people," she laughed. When she is finished with the administrative tasks, she goes home and lives her life; she is comfortable with it, even with its undemanding character.

But for some, I had the feeling these rules represent a minimalist reading of faith; the middle path becomes the path of least resistance. Jihn is serious about his Buddhism; he started a Buddhist club at school. But at the close of his interview he mused:

> Buddhists . . . are not really strict; it's more of a learning experience, I guess. A lesson in life or a way you could live your life that you could choose. Because we are not forced to go the temple or we are not Buddhists anymore. You don't have to pray or else you can't be a Buddhist. You don't have to sign papers . . . We believe in the Buddha and follow those five rules: don't lie, don't cheat . . . Eat three meals a day. Just really relaxed, like you [don't] have to do too much. It's more like a lazy thing for me.

Jihn is more honest than most, but I can imagine many Christians thinking about their faith in similar terms, even if they would not admit it publicly. Such responses made me reflect on the problems associated with a "cultured faith" in which thin belief can all too easily be correlated with thin practice.

By contrast, the typical elite response to questions about everyday life was to focus on the impact of meditation. Betty who is a part of ATS, and teaches there on Saturdays, was typical when she responded to such questions: "Buddhism is a lot about being in the present moment. So for me it's about being in the now." She thinks it is a way of life, rather than believing certain things or being religious. Buddha says you should "find out what's true for you." She sums up her views by noting Buddhism is "really about being mindful. And meditation is a training of the mind to be mindful and aware all the time. So it's, when you're sitting, know you're sitting. When you're walking, know you're walking . . ." When the mind is trained like this, she thinks, you can come and go, you can meditate no matter what is going on around you, "there's no distraction." Diane who grew up as a mainline Presbyterian, comes regularly to Hsi Lai and credits the practices there with making her a calmer person. In her prostrations, she says, "I'm humbling myself . . . I am letting [things] go, releasing them to the universe." When asked how this effects her life, she responded that she doesn't try to control things like she used to. "I think I let things and experiences happen and I don't let them affect as adversely . . . I accept things as they come and try to deal with them as they are. I feel a much more giving, caring, nurturing, compassionate person now. I was a very selfish person in the past . . . I think that I'm a much more giving person, with my time, especially." She credits Hsi Lai with facilitating this change. Not that coming there was magic, she says. But it allowed her to make changes in herself, and "because of those changes that I made, then that had the affect of things coming my way . . . because I was a changed person." Dan at Bodhi Path, who was raised as a Congregational Christian, thinks meditating causes one to focus on life, rather than doing what you are "knee jerked trained to do." He summed it up this way: "What I find, when I get home and I drive my vehicle and I take a breath, I am really focused and aware. I am not just going into the house, I am really aware of myself. I think that is what Buddha has taught me. Basically self-awareness rather than being caught up in my story. Basically, it breaks your ego—that is the purpose of it." Several others spoke similarly of applying this decentering and focusing oneself on life at home and with the family.

An especially interesting application of Buddhism to life is represented by Vibul, a monk who is also an artist at Wat Thai Temple. We interviewed him at his studio in Venice Beach. As a well-respected contemporary artist and a Thai Buddhist monk, Vibul occupies a strange middle ground between Western and Buddhist values. On the one hand, he works to apply his meditation to all of life, to get into the habit of "moving slowly," whether he is eating, driving, or painting. He likes the incense, candles, and flowers because they speak to him of his ancestors and culture (though none of this is necessary, he thinks, for higher level practice). On the other hand Vibul is conversant with Western art and struggles to see how he might incorporate it into his own work and his Buddhist values. He is especially drawn to modern art, because it is not simply imitation. "I can bring my soul into it," he says. A key theme in his own art is "coming in and going out," which applies the Buddhist teaching of things coming into existence and passing away—he wants to capture this in his art. As an extension of his meditation Vibul wants his art to be a visual trigger, like the images in the temple, to awakening one to the path of enlightenment. Interestingly though he is drawn to modern art, he pointedly avoids the modern view that art should be self-expression; indeed, for Vibul, it is to be a pointer toward effacement of the self.

Melanie and Kim who visit Hsi Lai both had evangelical Christian backgrounds. Melanie feels her experience at Hsi Lai has changed her life. She says: "Meditation helps me to look and examine the dissatisfaction I see with myself and others and really just examine that so I can really look at that deeply and look at the ways to stop that dissatisfaction or to resolve it . . . To have equanimity in my life, to be more joyful and then to share that with other people in my life too." Kim was deeply moved by his own bodhisattva vows, which he described as "living my life for others." He thinks being a dad, taking care of his children, has helped him understand that "my life is no longer mine, it is theirs." This gives him great joy. "Living my life to help others . . . [he searches for the right word] . . . what more is there?" Melanie and Kim have worked through the tension of meditation and their life in the world. They both love the peace of the temple, the wisdoms of the past and present, as Melanie put it, the forgetting of what's outside, as Kim says. Still they see this as changing them deeply on the inside so that life can be lived differently.

These thoughtful reflections, typical of other elite responses, made me reflect on especially the Protestant responses to questions about everyday life in our previous study. Protestant worship, which one respondent described as getting oneself "rebooted" for the week, is to promote a life of discipleship—following Christ, that extends into the whole of life. In fact the criterion for many Protestants for whether worship (or a sermon) is good, is whether it has a practical impact on everyday life, so that all of life becomes an act of worship.[4] There is obvious resonance here with the elite Buddhist responses we surveyed. But there are differences as well. While the Protestant responses made frequent reference to their working life— their worship changed the way they did their work. In the Buddhist sample, respondents rarely if ever made any direct application to work—though they frequently mention family and personal relationships. This resonance and this difference raise two issues for me.

First, as I hinted, there is a distinct difference in references to everyday life by ethnic and elite Buddhists. The former stressed the ethical side, the first step in the path to purification; the latter, though they would certainly not disagree with this emphasis, consistently stressed the mental formation of meditation and the influence of this on making them a more compassionate (i.e., mindful) person. What is the significance of these differences?

4. See Dyrness, *Senses of the Soul*, 125.

Two possibilities come to mind. Perhaps the influence of American culture, especially in its post-romantic therapeutic character, has stimulated these American Buddhists to think about their faith in the self-help terms of the larger culture. A related possibility is that the distinctly religious character of American culture might be impacting the practice of Buddhism. It is well known that religion in America is oriented toward a personal experience of God that is based on individual decision.[5] One wonders, especially in the case of Melanie and Kim, to what degree have their previous encounters with American evangelicalism colored their experience of Buddhism? Their understanding is no longer centered on God, of course, but it still bears the imprint of a search for personal faith. This search and its accompanying language, however, have now been relocated into their experience with Buddhism and the teachings they have received in the temple. Like the experience of Buddhists with Christian images or memories, this Christian past has been recontextualized into a Buddhist imagination.

Buddhist readers will judge for themselves whether these influences have resulted in a deviation from the tradition or an enrichment of it (Christians of course having their own analogous worries about the influence of American culture). But as a Christian, this discussion raises for me a further question: What is it that Melanie and Kim have found in their Buddhist practice that they, apparently, were not able to find in their Christian experiences? Are there lessons to be learned from the way these Buddhist respondents saw their practices forming dispositions, so that they were able to feel they were living transformed lives?[6]

5. I have explored this personal character of American religion in Dyrness, *How Does America Hear the Gospel?*

6. Such felt needs may account for the attraction younger Christians feel for some of the ancient Christian disciplines. See Gibbs and Bolger, *The Emerging Church.*

Chanting at Wat Thai Temple.

Conclusion: Being at Peace with Life and Death

From what we have learned from these voices, can we make some tenta-
tive suggestions about a possible Buddhist aesthetic? Any exposure to the
history of Buddhist art shows how difficult it is to generalize; indeed its images have ranged from the highly intricate and curvilinear forms of Hindu
inspired figures both in India and Southeast Asia, to the minimalism of the
Japanese Zen garden or the tea ceremony. But the frequency of references
to quieting the mind, ridding oneself of the monkey mind—the inces-
sant chattering associated with the external world, with its attractions and

distractions, suggest a common picture. The image that emerges, I would suggest, is to see these mental disciplines as chanting—a chanting that absorbs differences into itself and, working with them, harmonizes them. Buddhist practice is chanting one's life. Life shaped in this way can be seen as a melodious whole. I was struck by how persistent the refrain appeared that when one becomes competent in meditation (and chanting) one is able to discern a beauty in all things. If, as one respondent put it, Buddhism is about seeing things as they truly are, one can learn to accept them all with equanimity. One can be at peace.

Often reflections like this had a distinctly aesthetic character to them. Lama Khedrub, a teacher at Bodhi Path who is also an artist, recounted the way the bright colors of nature and of art (she especially loves Impressionist art) make her happy. Her meditation has produced a way of thinking that allows her to say: "I feel like art is everywhere. Art is about how I dress, how I dress my grandchildren . . . It's everywhere, in everything . . . I see it in the tree and the light, the play of light." Her testimony reflects how deeply her practice has filtered down into her life: "You know when you drive and the sky and the clouds and the way the light comes down, that moves me a lot. Certain paintings have this beautiful power to really take you out of yourself and out of your problems and worries and just remind you, life is bigger, that . . . there is so much beauty, so much to be grateful for, so why get stuck on stupid stuff?" Similarly Diane, who visits Hsi Lai says: "I try to find [beauty] wherever I go, in everything, and everybody that I meet."

Kim the former evangelical who has taken the bodhisattva vow at Hsi Lai connects this holistic vision with his experience of chanting. "It's just gorgeous. Sometimes when I go in and wear my robes and participate in one of the chanting services, that interaction is very special for me . . . visually it brings me into the present moment . . . mentally in that present moment being in that room." This present-ness enables him to see Buddha and the beauty of the Buddha everywhere. Venerable Miao Hsi elaborates the role art and beauty can play in engendering openness to life and its beauties: "[Art] opens my mind. It says that his world is so wonderful and there's a beautiful sight to everything." Later she claims art can help calm and focus the mind. "Over time it can become precious," especially, she notes, when it is connected to devotion. Otherwise it can be empty. "If you look at Buddhist art, it's not just art, it's also religion, it's also devotion."

If chanting prepares one to see beauty in the whole of life, it can also be said to prepare one to die. The impulse to see life holistically led several respondents to reflect on their faith as a preparation for their death. An important part of Buddhist practice is designed to promote serenity even in the face of death. Pablo, the Catholic who came to the U.S. from Lima, Peru, could speak of his practice as "preparing the vessel, preparing these moments for the moment of death." Hoshi of Zen Soto Mission recalls her first visual memory, visiting the grave of her family members, something that she immediately connected with the altar in her home. She first came to the temple for the funeral of her mother and father-in-law. Now she attends regularly and volunteers and finds it a place of deep beauty. When asked what role the space plays in her meditation, she replied: "You know I'm living now, but some day I die and will have the funeral service here. Then even after my death, I will be here and people will see me here, and think and remember . . . that is the role of space." For these the space of the temple becomes that place where, in meditation and chanting, the connections between things are forged, a kind of second home, where one comes to learn to be quiet, to volunteer, to live, and finally to die.

The wisdom represented by Buddhism in the face of death is moving, and it is represented by, for example, the reclining Buddha, who expresses his serenity in the face of death, but its images are contrasted by the very different Christian understandings of death and the images associated with it. The Buddhist wisdom is reflected in an ancient folktale. Phra one of the young monks at Wat Thai recounted the story of the rich woman during Buddha's life whose baby died. She was distraught and sought out a doctor who might be able to revive the baby. He said, I can do nothing, but go to the Buddha maybe he can help you. When Buddha heard about the baby's death, he told the woman. "I can make a drug that will treat the baby, but I have to mix it with a certain seed. Go find and bring me this seed, but you cannot take it from any house in which a person has died." She went and frantically tried to find the seed in a house where no one had died, but of course she could not find any such house. Then she understood, there is no house free of death. She came back to the Buddha to say she understood, and later became the first female monk.

This then is the Buddhist wisdom that was so widely evident in the voices we have heard—a wisdom of openness to what is and a refusal to accept any illusions about life, coupled with a deep conviction that all sentient creatures would one day realize the Buddha nature. This produced a particular aesthetic of peace and acceptance that I have likened to chanting one's life. Here perhaps we can suggest the difference between this way and the aesthetic orientation of Christianity. The voices in our sample several times made reference to one Christian image that seemed incapable of being absorbed into the Buddhist imagination: Christ on the cross. Venerable Maio Hsi went to a Catholic school in Hong Kong, and though she has become a Buddhist, the images from her past stay with her. She says of her Catholic schooling: "Every classroom has a crucifix of Jesus hanging there. You know, that is a very strong image." The Virgin Mary, she goes on to say is kind and motherly and is like images that exist in Buddhism. But the crucifix is something unmistakably different. Mako would agree with her assessment. Though baptized as a Presbyterian when a toddler, he has come to be a part of the Zen Soto Temple—becoming active when his Buddhist parents passed away. He volunteers, we recall, to make the temple a better place for everyone. Meditation calms him down. But when asked what religious image most deeply moves him, he answers: Christ on the cross. "I still have this image of Christ being crucified on the cross . . . that is very sad for someone." He went on to acknowledge how similar the teachings of Christianity and Buddhism are, the Ten Commandments and the percepts of Buddha. But there is a difference that cannot be captured in this kind of comparison—it is, in part, an aesthetic difference. Mako put it this way, immediately after making the preceding comparisons: "But as far as images go, like I said, it was very depressing to see Christ on the cross, you know. That image was . . . still haunts me."

That haunting image according to the apostle Paul is the substance of Christian message, though he acknowledges it is for many people unsettling: "We proclaim Christ crucified, a stumbling block to Jews and foolishness to Gentiles" (1 Cor 1:23). Still, he insists this represents another kind of wisdom: "to those who are the called both Jews and Greeks, Christ the power of God and the wisdom of God" (v. 24). Indeed even for many Christians the image of the cross is painful. But, strangely, it also is central to what might be called a Christian aesthetic. Christian believers can even claim to see an awful beauty in the cross. Theologian John de Gruchy proposes that "in some mysterious way this corrupt world is redeemed by the beauty concealed in the crucified Christ."[7] Perhaps there is beauty hidden, as it were, in the cross, in "the manner in which God's goodness gives itself and is expressed by God and understood by man as the truth."[8] Though the wisdom and beauty are only to be found in the larger complex of events and

7. De Gruchy, *Christianity*, 101.
8. Ibid., 104.

meanings in which the cross is oriented, it is central to the way Christians imagine their lives.

Clearly the difficulty that the Buddhist respondents have with this image reflects not simply a difference of belief about death. It speaks of a stubbornly different imagination. Mei, who returned to her ancestral Buddhist faith after coming to America from Taiwan, expressed this difference. The big difference she sees between Buddhism and Christianity is that Christians "have to have Jesus which helps you . . . be able to be with God." But Buddha, she says, when enlightened found "that all the sentient beings . . . have the Buddha nature and so have to understand and work to perfect ourselves to become Buddha . . . You don't have to go through Jesus or anybody and we have to start correcting it ourselves." She even sees a parallel between the way Americans all depend on pills to save them, when the best way is "to watch your diet, exercise and have a happy mind." We have to walk the walk, she says. And the walk reflects the discipline that seeks liberation from distorting emotions and an acceptance of life and death. On the other hand, the "sad death" of Jesus speaks of another complex of affections and practices that can only be understood in terms of a Christian imagination.

In the Christian celebration of the first Sunday in Advent, pastors wear colorful stoles, and the sanctuary is decorated with flowers. The music and the readings focus on the expectation of what the prophets described as the end of history. The Gospel reading for the day speaks of people "fainting from fear and foreboding of what is coming upon the world," and so we are exhorted to "be on guard so that your hearts are not weighed down with dissipation and drunkenness and the worries of this life" (Luke 21:26, 34). My Buddhist friends would feel at home with such instructions but not with the fear and clearly not with the foreboding that Mary came to feel over a son whose vocation included death. The narrative shapes how Christians seek to live out their precepts. Buddhist practices suggest a different narrative. There are resonances, visual overlap, and mutual illumination between the practices and the impulses of these faiths, and a critical aspect of these resonances, and of the differences, so I am arguing, is aesthetic.

Entrance to Imam Center.

Islam, Worship, and Beauty

The Touch and Feel of Muslim Piety

In the church where we worship, the pastor comes down the center aisle to read the Gospel lesson while the congregation stands—to symbolize that, in Christ, God came into our world. During the reading I imagine Christ with his disciples and the people, teaching them. Muslims also hear recitations of their sacred text, the Quran, during their worship. But they are less likely to imagine Muhammad receiving the text from Gabriel, than to picture the text itself—its shape, its words. For Muslim believers hearing, seeing, and touching the Quran are enriching practices.

In fact the dominant impression we received from our respondents was the importance of the actual physical touch and feel of their practices— that is the five pillars, which they believe connect them to each other and to God. They readily spoke of seeing and touching the Quran, the feel of washing before prayers, the touch of others praying alongside, even the soft feeling of the carpet on which they pray. On one level this is a surprising finding, given the strict iconoclasm associated with the tradition. Absolutely no image of any creature, not of Muhammad certainly nor of God, are allowed, for worship is the direct, unmediated connection of worshipers with God. It is the pursuit of oneness (tawhid). Yet, in spite of this pursuit of a pure connection with God, time and again they spoke of the physical connections they treasured in their experience of prayer.

The Quran is central to Muslim worship, because it represents not simply a message from God, but the very voice of God. As a result, its presence is tangible for Muslims. In fact when asked what image had an impact on their spiritual life, several immediately mentioned seeing the Quran or a page from the Quran. Gordon, an African American who worships at the Islamic Center of Southern California, sees a book or a page that represents to him his unquenchable desire to learn. Kaliq from Ibad Allah when asked the same question responded: "A page of the Quran. That's really my whole spiritual life because I am forced to look at it . . . going to class, now I went to class yesterday and it gives you a page to memorize. So you're forced to look at this page for like a few hours, before going back and testing with the page, so that's really the image that I have in my head. I have a page in my head at all times. That's my image." Naim Shaw, an assistant imam at Ibad Allah, when asked about memories of religious imagery from his childhood, remembered putting portions from the Quran on the wall and the Quran open. "You'll find the Quran opened, you know, like opened, like an image of the book. It was always red, like a red background with a green book opened." He says you will see this image everywhere, but it stands out from his childhood. He thinks these images "painted the picture within, you know, kind of added to a sense of identity and purpose or maybe helping me be a little more rooted." He has these images in his home now so his children will have this experience.

When asked about religious imagery, Mufti of the Islamic Center of Southern California (ICSCA), thinks of the calligraphic style of the text—something that came up frequently. The actual Arabic writing for many is an impressive and moving image. Though his father was Muslim, Mufti's mother was a Methodist so he had to make a conscious choice to follow Islam when growing up. As he learned more about it, he says, "my focus was on the Quran, reading it, memorizing it . . . And it was through looking at the script, and the way it looked on the page that—as opposed to an image of God, for example—it was through the beauty of the calligraphy that I found an expression of spirituality." Nero is also a convert—he grew up in Mexico in a Catholic family and converted five years before we interviewed him. Seeing calligraphy of verses of the Quran gives him a sense of "urgent beauty"; it inspires in him the need to read and understand more. Farhana of the ICSCA admitted that she, like Nero, struggles to read the Arabic of the Quran, though she loves to look at it. "It looks like poetry, like art poetry," she says.

Reading the Quran at Masjid Ibad Allah

Farhana's struggle to understand what she is reading is not untypical. Since all recitations and prayers are in Arabic, most Muslims who do not speak Arabic in the home try to learn enough Arabic to follow along. Since the understanding is imperfect, therefore, the impact of the readings and recitations is primarily oral and visual. For this reason one might argue that the encounter with the text is necessarily aesthetic rather than cognitive—or at least it is aesthetic before it is cognitive. When our researcher asked Mimar, who works as a counselor at the Orange County Islamic Foundation (OCIF), whether he could understand the calligraphy that was painted throughout the mosque, he admitted that he looked for a key word that he could make out. "If you can find one key word, then you will probably know what verse in the Quran that the whole piece is saying." Though he "respects" the use of calligraphy and can appreciate it, he is more deeply moved by the recitation itself— by what is heard, rather than what is seen. Aasif who does the call to prayers at Idad Allah reported that during Salat he stays focused on the words. "Believe it or not, while you're making Salat, you can see . . . the Arabic words coming by, you can actually see the letters as the words go by . . . so that calligraphy is pretty powerful."

Calligraphy on the walls of Mission Viejo Mosque

Since the Quran represents the presence of God's words—a transcription of his voice—one must carefully prepare oneself to touch it. Thus the ritual washing, or ablution, is a necessary prelude to the prayers and a place is set aside for this in every mosque. Nashmia, a young mother, grew up in

Afghanistan—with Islam but not in Islam, as she says. It was not until she came to America that she seriously began to practice her faith, at the Iman Center in Palms. When asked about what religious imagery she connects with her faith, she immediately responded: "The Holy Quran, the book itself represents a very sacred piece of art." The actual book itself, the interviewer asked? "Yeah," she responded, "you have to wash before you touch the holy Quran or you read it. So, it prepares you spiritually . . . You have to actually spiritually prepare, and you have to wash and you have to be cleaned [sic] of all evils, meaning of all, any kind of physical dirt." Only when you have cleansed yourself from these distractions, worries, or unholy thoughts, then "when you read the Quran, you have some kind of peace of mind. It grounds you and . . . you say, OK, I trust God, and something good is going to happen." Significantly it seems that the reading itself—the oral recitation of the Quran, carries the blessing in addition to the specific message that it contains. Indeed one might say the blessing resides in the whole process of encountering the text, the pattern of practices that include the call to prayer, the ablution, the recitation, the prostration, and so on.

Naim Shaw speaks memorably of this pattern as the *etiquette* of prayer, which "you can employ . . . and it would enhance your remembrance." It even starts before you arrive at the mosque, when you can say a prayer to prepare yourself. He says: "That's the etiquette, you know. The etiquette of having a good scent on you, so they have oils around . . . [that] you might want to put [on] . . . The incense sometimes . . . does it. And I guess the different artwork that's on the walls provides that. But if you're not familiar with all these etiquettes, then the experience will not be as intense." This etiquette Naim has had to learn and appropriate over the years, it helps him cultivate a sense of being with God in prayer. Edina is a third-generation American of Ethiopian descent, who prays at the King Fahad Mosque in Culver City. When asked when she felt closest to God, she responded, when she washes up before prayer. "It's like I'm washing from head to toe . . . You can't rush through it. You know part of your prayer is . . . purity and cleanliness and there's so much ritual that's involved and you can't even skimp around becoming pure. So I feel my prayer begins there, that the fact that I'm really only fearing God at that point."

Rajah who is from Sudan and prays at King Fahad stresses the physical nature of the cleanliness he seeks. The Prophet Muhammad spoke of this, Rajah pointed out. Your clothes should be clean, your breath should not smell "because the angels wouldn't feel comfortable with that, and the mosque is filled with angels. So [Muhammad] talked on so many occasions about the importance of being clean. In fact, he said, cleanliness is [a] big part of the belief, so that gives it extra importance." Cleanliness is connected to belief, for Rajah; indeed it is a singular expression of belief. External cleanliness is a corollary of internal purity; it facilitates and enhances one's prayer. But note that the feeling of being united with God is driven by the act of washing. Ablution, as a part of the larger pattern of practices, becomes itself an act of prayer that carries an intrinsic spirituality for these Muslims.

The pattern of practice, the etiquette, begins formally with ablution but continues in the prayers and with the recitation of portions of the Quran by the imam—or the person leading the prayers (often simply a male lay leader). As in the ritual washing, it seems that the focus of worshipers is on the performance rather than the message. When reflecting on the visual things associated with her praying, Edina, like Aasif, says that she is starting to "visualize the Quran, as I recite it. Because I'm trying to be closer to it, and trying to memorize [a] lot more. And seeing it I kind of see it in my mind's eye when I'm praying." Seeing it in this way is an important way for her to feel closer to it. Sinam was born and raised in Pakistan and prays at King Fahad. He is deeply moved by reciting God's words. "You have the honor," he thinks, "of actually uttering the same exact words . . . the text, the visual aspect is what was revealed. That's about as close as I can get to [God's] speech." Pui Lan who prays with her family at OCIF confessed that during her prayers she pictures the calligraphy of the Arabic word "Allah."

For Muslims the recitation of the Quran is a spiritual practice, but, they would all agree, it is also makes an aesthetic impact. Someone who is good at recitation is honored (Muslims even have yearly international competitions for the best Qari, or cantor, of the Quran). Gordon, the African American raised in Iowa, thinks in fact that recitation is the ultimate form of poetry. When growing up he loved hip-hop—for him art and spirituality were inseparable. He still remembers the impression Quranic recitation made on him when he first heard it. He thought: "Wow! This rappin' in Arabic is the fliest [sic] thing I ever heard!"

Shehla is the twentysomething wife of the imam in the Mission Viejo Mosque (OCIF), who was raised in Dubai until age twelve. She voiced the typical Islamic concern for images: "We don't have pictures for Islamic symbols, people, nothing, nothing at all." But she is deeply moved by the recitation of the Quran in her mosque. One of the imams has a fine voice,

she says: "When he recites . . . he makes you concentrate in the prayer because . . . his voice helps you." She thinks you feel passages more because
Allah revealed them in rhythm, "so when you recite them in a certain way,
you feel them more." So the quality of the recitation, she thinks, matches
the mood of Allah's voice. Yasmia prays at the same mosque in Mission
Viejo (OCIF), and moved to the U.S. from India when she was eight years
old. She also loves the recitation of this cantor. She says: "It's so intoxicating
. . . and you just close your eyes, and, at least when I close my eyes and everything I just really feel like crying. I don't understand a word of what he's
saying, but the depth of his voice and the way he goes high and low pitch
. . . so that's another attraction for me to come around [the mosque]." The
physical sound of the cantor makes this worshiper feel the presence of God.
Her testimony confirms the view of the Muslim scholar Seyyed Hossein
Nasr: "Muslims live in a space defined by the sound of the Quran."[1]

This resonates with one of the few studies that seeks to describe the
role of aesthetics and beauty in Muslim and Christian worship. George
Dardess and Peggy Rosenthal have sought to describe the differing ways
beauty functions in these traditions. In his discussion of the *adhan*, or call
to prayer, Dardess, after himself practicing the *adhan* for two weeks, con-
cludes "that in the *adhan* I was hearing the true art of Muslims, and even
the first historical example—as well as the epitome—of their art."[2] This is
because the call responds (and articulates) what is beautiful in the Quran
itself.

As the recitation represents the aural presence of God, so their physical prostrations, the response to this voice, connect Muslims to God. When
Farhana was asked what aspects of her prayers encourage the sense of God's
presence, she replied: "The actual act of prayer I think. Like sitting on the
ground with your hands on your knees, yeah, that's I think [the] moment
of prayer where I feel that [presence]." When pressed why this is so, she
thought it was the stillness. But "also in some sense in doing yoga or in
doing anything else that is physical and still and focused, that forces you
to slow down." Stillness, a sense of presence, slowing down—all these are
mediated by the physical activity of praying. This focus on the physical is
especially evident in what is called prostration, when Muslim worshipers

1. *IS I*, 4.

2. Dardess and Rosenthal, *Reclaiming Beauty for the Good of the World*, 69. Interestingly, though they are able to connect beauty with the actual practices of Muslim worship,
when they come to Christian beauty the discussion moves to the broader experience and
construal of life.

lower their heads and touch their forehead to the ground. Kaliq from Ibad Allah, in response to the question of when he feels closest to God, spoke for many others when he said: "When you are prostrating, when your forehead face is touching the ground—you are at the humblest point. It removes arrogance." All are equal, whether royalty or commoner, all acknowledge at that moment that God is in control, Kaliq says. At that moment of touching the ground, Muslims believe the distance between the believer and Allah is overcome.

Prostration at Masjid Ibad Allah

It would be wrong to give the impression that Muslims do not think deeply about these practices or that they have only a formal meaning for them. We will see how articulate some can be about what these things mean to them. But clearly it is the practice that dominates. Notice how frequently these respondents can refer to their emotional (and aesthetic) response to prayers, or to the writing of the Quran, even when they do not understand what is said or understand it only with difficulty. The direction of the movement of worship is from external practices to internal meanings. It is not the case that Edina prays for cleanliness and submits to ablution as an *expression* of this commitment, rather she carefully follows the prescribed rituals, and in the course of—and *as a result of* these she feels closer to God. Christians are apt to find this focus on the physical practices off-putting, as the proper order of worship for them is from within outward. Doesn't reversing this order, they wonder, risk making ritual primary to faith? It might do so, given the Christian understanding of faith. But perhaps, when we understand these practices in terms of a broader Muslim imagination—their religious imaginary, the logic of this order will become clear.

The Disciplines of Knowing God

To move us toward such a broader understanding we might ask how these respondents understand their relationship with God. How is this imagined? Time and time again respondents spoke of prayer as connecting them to God and that spirituality is something that takes place not externally but within themselves. They frequently emphasized that the Muslim faith is about the absolute surrender to God, becoming one with God. In spite of the importance, even priority, given to physical practices, all would agree that the goal is the inner connection with God. Sadegh Namazikhah the director of the Iman Center describes the importance of prayer. Muslims repeat in their prayers: "Oh God, lead us in the righteous way," he notes. "And I think in reality, this is a commitment. You ask for something but at the same time you make a commitment . . . I feel that if I'm asking for something, in the time of giving a commitment to it and if you give it to me, I'm going to follow it." Abdul from Masjid Abad Allah agrees. He feels closest to God during salat, the regular ritual prayers. During this time you pray for knowledge or forgiveness. But then, he says, you need to "pick it up with you and put it on your back, and move towards that goal." He believes that if you walk toward your prayer, the creator will open the door for you. This inner commitment based, as some said on taqwa (the consciousness of God), is the central focus of their piety. Their practice is meant to encourage, nurture, and deepen this inward orientation.

As a result most respondents, though they can appreciate the calligraphy and other forms of Muslim art, insisted these played no direct role in their prayers. Usman who is director of the King Fahad Mosque summed up this attitude toward the end of his interview. You keep asking about images, he finally said. "We don't have imagery." There are some traditions like the Sufi mystics or dervishes from Turkey who may talk more about the "physical part you are looking for. For us, it's . . . the connection [that] comes from within and imagery has no place. When it comes to religion, there's a one-on-one with God, no intercession, no intermediaries [like the

Catholic Church] . . . My salvation does not lie in accepting another person as a sacrifice for my sins . . . So we cut out the middleman. We're not after the symbols . . . I reach God through the book he has revealed and through His words." The problem for Usman seems to lie with the fact that symbols and images are all things that humans have made; as a result they are of no use in our salvation. God alone is the source of this salvation and nothing should compete with God's power. Mimar, from Eritrea, came to the U.S. for his education and now prays with his young family at the Mission Viejo Mosque. He emphasized that "religiosity is something that resides in your heart" and that can only be expressed in your character. Visual images and objects are not encouraged because they make no contribution to the orientation of one's heart. Mimar developed this in two ways. First there is always the fear that one can fall into pride or hypocrisy by depending on visual imagery—people can depend on these things and not develop the character that is necessary. But more important, he stressed, is the fact that since religion is a matter of the heart, any external mediation or influence necessarily undercuts this inner focus. The most vital aspect is "the personal efforts that the person puts in order to attain their own spiritual growth, rather than just having to be dependent on some outside source." The use of "visual expressions of faith" implies, to Mimar, dependence on some outside source.

Mimar and others we interviewed seemed intent on making a sharp distinction, when it came to their worship, between the physical practices central to their faith and other artistic or symbolic expressions of faith. The first are revered, the second call for careful discipline. This leads observers to say that Islam is better understood as aniconic rather than iconoclastic.[3] But even this way of putting things stresses what Islam does without, rather than what it recommends. Perhaps it is better to suggest the Muslim imagination shapes a positive program of ritual practices that is understood to promote the inward surrender to God. What do the framed images of calligraphic verses from the Quran do for him, we asked Nero, the Mexican convert? He replied: "They act as a reminder of my duties as a person of faith." Naim Shaw gave perhaps the best explanation of this constructive focus of Muslim faith. He noted that, in worship, he responds most deeply to the particular Arabic words of the prayers, or the attributes of God (others agreed adding the written name of Allah or Muhammad). "Because you don't have an image of God in Islam," he explained, "then the imagery that

---

3. Cf. Titus Burckhardt, "The Spirituality of Islamic Art," 520.

is formed is [the] understanding of his words." It is, he thinks, intellectual. "Something birthed through knowledge."

For a Christian observer this response might suggest that Muslims get knowledge from the Quran in the way Christians get their knowledge from Scripture. But I believe such a comparison would be mistaken. The extensive evidence for the primary role that practices play—which, after all, are very physical and even visual—suggests that the knowledge to which Naim refers is very different from what Christians think of as knowledge. In general when Christians talk about what they believe, the knowledge associated with faith, they refer to a set of events and their interpretations described in the Bible that are to be believed—things usually put in the form of a creed or confession. I believe Naim's use of knowledge is closer to the understanding of knowledge in the Hebrew Scriptures, where it is a holistic orientation expressive of a relationship—as in the man "knew his wife" and they became one flesh.[4] To know God, for Muslims is to be properly oriented toward God, to the creation, and to others. This orientation, expressed and developed in the practices we have reviewed, is a central component of a Muslim imagination.

But one might still press the question What exactly do the practices do? How do they do their work of promoting the surrender to God? It is interesting that Usman should suggest that Sufism might stress more the physical aspect that mainstream Islam rejects. Though our sample of Sufi respondents was small (two identified themselves as Sufi and several others acknowledged the influence of Sufism), our respondents seemed to dispute this suggestion. Jumaana was raised in the home of a filmmaker in Turkey, and now living in Los Angeles, has followed in her father's footsteps. After passing through an atheist period in college she visited the Kabah and realized, when she saw the image of crowds spinning around that sacred spot, that "there is some faith." This led her to embrace Sufism as the quest, as she put it, to face herself and connect with "good energy." She feels you can't simply do this "through your prayer in Islam" (she doesn't go regularly to the mosque), rather this connection is what is sought in all religions and can be found in many ways. For her it is best realized sitting in meditation, perhaps in a mosque or even a church—"Because when the people pray

---

4. See Genesis 4:1 et al. Cf. Titus Burckhardt's comment: "The Muslim soul and thereby Islamic art are grounded in a world that is closer to that of the Old Testament patriarchs than to the Greco-Roman universe" ("The Spirituality of Islamic Art," 511).

there they leave good energy." She associates this with being spiritual, but "since an artist must be attached to her roots," she still calls herself Muslim.

Picture of Kabah at Imam Center

Matthew was raised in India in the Mahdavi tradition of Islam (those who wait for the coming of the Mahdi, or messiah). During college he too left his strict background behind and eventually came to the States. In San Pedro, California he had a mystical encounter that he had trouble fitting into his previous religious experience. He called it God because that was what people expected, but it troubled him. Eventually, after reading about various religions, he identified himself as a Sufi, because, he says, "I could see that Sufi model could absorb all of the religions or could include all of them." Now he teaches and writes about Sufism. He is still a Muslim, he insists—Sufis are invariably Muslim, he notes. But Sufis do not necessarily practice the five pillars. He explained how this could be: "Five pillars is not Islam. I mean it's not really totally Islam. You can observe the five pillars . . . [but] praying five times a day does not make you a Muslim . . . Zakat does not make you a Muslim. None of these things make you a Muslim. What makes you a Muslim is surrendering your life to the service of God, to the service of humanity." What about reciting the Shahada—"There is no God but God and Muhammad is His Prophet"—isn't that essential, we asked? "But how seriously are you taking that statement? That is the key," he responded. "[Does] just reciting it make you a Muslim or believing that and internalizing that makes you a Muslim?" So it is the fact of surrender that matters; the practices, he thinks, are secondary. In fact he has studied a lot of "methodologies" and all are potentially useful. But his model is the Prophet Muhammad himself, or even the prophet Jesus; they were the best examples of Sufis!

These Sufi respondents seem to sever the strong connection that most respondents make between the fact of surrender and the practices that express this. Praying in a mosque or a church or beside the ocean may stimulate the sense of surrender to God, they believe, but such practices do not *necessarily* do so.[5] Similarly neither of these respondents made any direct connection between art and their religious experience. In some ways Protestant Christians can sympathize with such a view—in fact it is not difficult to find Christians making similar statements about praying in church or partaking of the sacraments. On the one hand, it is not hard to see how becoming overly dependent on the ritual practice can become barren and unreflective. On the other hand it is difficult to see how, in Islam, these practices can be so important and enriching for so many when their intrinsic value is questioned. How do Muslims seek to negotiate this tension? To answer this question we need to explore other themes arising from the Muslim responses.

The Beauty of Creation and the Role of Art

If anything can be said with certainty about Muslim practice it is this: Muslim faith is fundamentally about a proper orientation toward God. Islam (from the Arabic word meaning "submission") is about surrendering oneself to the will of God. This fundamental orientation determines Muslim attitudes toward the beauty of the created order and the possibilities (and limitations) of art, and even the appropriate role of religious practice. One of our questions asked about their experience with art and what art they liked best. Many in fact had some experience and even training in art (perhaps because they volunteered knowing we were interested in art and images). But Mimar from the Mission Viejo (OCIF) mosque insisted, along

5. Sufis even seem to qualify the singularity of Muhammad, rather stressing his role as the last of the great prophets. Cf. "The Koran specifically says that God makes no distinction among prophets or Messengers of God; they are all of equal status" (Abdallah, *A Sufi's Rumination*, 78).

with others, that his first inclination was to see beauty in nature: "Your job is to reflect, to ponder, and to reason, and to enjoy the beauty of what God has enjoyed." In fact whenever you see something beautiful you should say, "Praise the Lord who has created such beauty."

When asked where they experienced beauty most often, the common response was in nature. Though this answer was typical across all the religious traditions that we have explored, Muslims gave a particular reason for this. Enjoying creation pushes you to "give credit to the One who made beauty possible, and that would be God," as Mimar put it. Naim Shaw believes that in nature the "majesty of God just explodes." Shafiq thinks anything in nature, even a dog, can make you feel connected to God. Sinam, who was born and raised in Pakistan and has studied architecture, put this into the larger context of Muslim worship. He noted that design and creativity, things that are important to him, suggest something beyond what he can understand. He explained: "This is the concept of infinity. What is it? [It is] mind-boggling to think about it, and that's where you submit, that's the end and extent of intellect, to where you submit, so that's what it's all about. You are submitting to God because He's created you, and He's given you all these things." Quoting a verse from the Quran, Sinam notes that God gave these things to people "until they submit." Daniel at Masjid Al Taqwa described creation as a grand object lesson for people: "[Allah] taught the apple tree to grow the apple, and . . . taught the bird to fly, so, you know, everything has what we call a natural fitra, a natural way . . . so you know if we go by what God has taught us and has written in so many places . . . it takes away all that other confusion. It takes away, you know, the risk."

Edina, who teaches psychology and was interviewed at King Fahad, is drawn to the beauty of nature, especially the colors of fruit, leading her to enjoy textiles and rugs made with these colors. Though she is moved by colors and their reflection in the rugs and decoration of the mosque (King Fahad has designs that look like trees on the front walls), this does "not play a[s] big a role in my prayers as the action." The point is, she says, coming to the mosque we are obeying the commandment of God and that "we return to him several times a day, to have these standard prayers, and that our lives are structured on this, and that we've submitted to this, and we all see the beauty in it." "All this has structured our lives" could serve as a kind of refrain whenever respondents spoke about their religious practices. These provided an order and an orientation for their lives. And for many this structure itself provides a kind of ordered beauty.

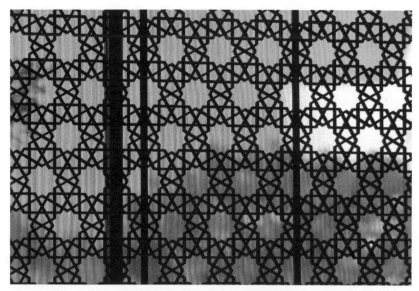

Window at a mosque in Mission Viejo

This is not to say the actual art of Islam, in all of its rich historical manifestations, is not important to these Muslims. Many commented on the fact that this cultural tradition makes them proud and grounds their sense of belonging. Farhana confessed that art plays a big role in her life. In fact, she says, "that's why I continue to be a religious person." But the "art" that connects her spiritually is embodied in her ritual practices. In fact Farhana, who admitted earlier that the calligraphy of the Quran is "like poetry, art poetry," insisted that the importance of this is "reconnecting with the Quran and with God's message and with yourself . . . but [there's a lot she doesn't understand] because Arabic is not . . . a familiar language to me . . . it's almost an art to me." The art facilitates the connection with the words of God, which, acted out in her prayers, helps to structure her life, even beyond what she can properly understand.

Needless to say art plays a major role in many traditions of Islam— some mentioned Persian miniatures, others the architecture of Moorish Spain. Some respondents could even articulate a framework for a fairly compelling understanding of art in relation to their faith. Omar who came to the U.S. from Pakistan in the seventies claimed that he is more into writing than the visual arts but enjoys the beauty of nature. When asked whether an image from the Quran or calligraphy contributed to his prayers. He answered: "When you see [a] painting, someone who is not religious or someone who does not relate to religion would say, 'Oh, that's just [a] bunch of trees, a lake, mountains, a couple of boats.' But I would imagine that I would . . . think [of] it as God created these mountains and those lakes and the trees." Even when you think about a human being, he says, "Wow, if you just look at a human being, it's [sic] a masterpiece." But if you did not keep in mind that God created these wonders, even "things like painting would not really be of value to you." So art has a value only insofar as it reflects and encourages the connection that all things have to God. But while this connection is reflected in these images, it is not *created* by them; this role is reserved for the special practices that constitute the five pillars.

The Structure of Everyday Life

How then to these practices structure the time of Muslim believers? What is their impact on everyday life? Saif was born and raised in Iran and is drawn to the ascetic mysticism of the Sufi tradition. At the (Shiite) Iman Center he especially loves the Thursday night supplication when the lights are turned off, candles are lit, and they chant. They join in a prayer originally offered by the Imam Ali, the fourth caliph. Saif feels that darkness is "the most visual awakening sense, for in it is the idea of seclusion with God." At that moment, he says, tears roll down his face and that of many others in the congregation. Later, when asked what aspects of prayers have the most impact on his daily life, he answers: "The discipline of actually doing the prayers. The discipline that one has to go through by rising up early in the morning and the thoughtfulness of the hours which is brought to you by God through doing all the prayers. Everyday the prayers are to be done." Others commented that these five daily prayers organize their lives, remind them of their connection with God, and who they are. Shahed thinks "you need those five breaks in a day, just to stop, to think, to reflect in a way that I don't otherwise unless I am praying."

Part of this is the intrinsic satisfaction of connecting with God during the prayer. Kaliq thinks that the salat (ritual prayers) in general are important but the early morning prayer is specially meaningful, because you are not getting up to go to work for money, "only Allah gets you up." When most people are asleep, you are worshiping Allah. This is a great privilege. "You feel it as a special station and Allah has placed you in it and you feel privileged." This gives him a feeling of joy. When he is reading religious poetry or singing (which is included in the prayers at Iman Center), Saif feels "that I'm closer to God, you know . . . I can spiritually feel that I'm getting closer to God." Elsewhere Saif even likens this to a sense of being released from an involvement in the material world, as he says, it allows you "to loose up your spirit"—a feeling that recalls the goal of Buddhist meditation.

But another part of the regular prayers is the awakening sense of accountability they brings, what several respondents referred to as jihad, the struggle with oneself. As Nashmia put it, the goal is "to lead your life in a peaceful manner." Yasmin was even more explicit in her description of this struggle. "I think I'm a little partly good at being God-conscious, but I still do my own evil things . . . there are so many things that I'm supposed to be doing that I don't do." When she was in India she doesn't think she was nearly as God-conscious as she is in the U.S. "I think America got me . . . closer to God." For Muslims the sense of accountability is underlined by the certainty that they will one day stand before God to give account of their life. Jamal from Iman Center came from Iran thirty years ago but only recently returned to the mosque. He struggles to pay attention to the words and meanings of the prayers because he is deeply concerned about the next life. So much so that he says "nothing . . . much of this life interests me." For this reason he pays great attention to his five daily prayers. Nashmia also thinks about the next life when she prays. In fact when asked what role visual elements play in her prayers she answered that she tries to keep focused on God. "But for me, often when I pray, I remember death actually. It leads me to the life hereafter. I often think of how life would be when I die, and how peaceful would it be and where would I be and that's my personal imagery." She admitted that she had never shared this with anyone. Adib works with the youth at OCIF. When asked when he experiences God most deeply, he said when he visited Mecca and when his grandfather died. He was close to his grandfather and, he said, "being present when you see a life going from here to like leaving is definitely . . . you definitely feel like you're in the presence of God, like it's just unquestionable. You're like okay that life was here, and that person was warm and breathing and then like now they're gone, and you know that they're never coming back." He thought about God and spirituality for a long time after that.

For some, the image of actually standing before God comes frequently to their mind. In fact Mufti often thinks of this when he stands in the mosque during prayers. He tells us: "There is the imagery of the standing before God on the day of judgment . . . and we'll be standing before God to account for . . . so I kind of envision myself when I am standing before God in prayer, silent—it's a time to reflect upon what . . . that accounting will be like." This image plus the physical act of prostrating himself before God, he thinks, "opens a door in my heart to let my emotions pour out, and let . . . my connection to God strengthen." The image becomes part of the event of prayer and deepens his sense of oneness with God. Tanim from King Fahad also likes to visualize the day of judgment. He says, "I imagine if I'm standing in front of God in front of all these billions of people . . . who have died . . . I envision this." This helps orient him onto the right path. Later he tells us that the regular prayers daily help him organize his life, but they also hold him accountable: "If you have a habit of lying . . . that's my weakness . . . if you're praying to God five times a day, it's a reminder you shouldn't be doing this."

Window/skylight at Orange County Islamic Foundation

In spite of the stricture about images, many admitted mental images like these came to them during prayers. Interestingly, many spoke of working to stay focused, not looking around and so on, indicating how frequently images (and other distractions) intruded—a worry that many Protestant Christians would share. One young woman, Sara, who was born in Iran and came to the U.S. seven years ago, spoke of the tranquility and peace of the mosque. She likes to close her eyes, "when I'm very determined, then

I am really focused." She admitted that she used to think of God as an old man with white hair, who is kind like her papa, "but now I'm trying to remove that image and I'm trying actually to empty my mind." Rajah insisted that he kept his mind blank while praying—art is totally irrelevant here, he assured us. Rajah recalled that the Prophet Muhammad himself said the "quality of prayer is its mental attendance." When he prays, we asked Rajah, what visual images come in to his mind? Nothing, zero, my mind is blank, he insisted. But he immediately went on to say that to help him focus he imagines "paradise on my right hand, and I imagine hell on my left. I imagine the narrow path in the middle . . . It's like a bridge, but it's like really narrow and dangerous." These images may not be like art in his mind, but they are still graphic carriers of emotional weight. And they remind us how difficult, and fraught, is the project of suppressing images. But they also suggest that images, when they are present, emerge, unbidden, in the performance of the stipulated practices and in this way promote and support those practices.

These confessions give us an idea of the impact of prayer on everyday life—after listening to these we can imagine them working for peace, following the narrow path of honesty, and so on. But strangely, as was the case with the Buddhist respondents, there were few actual descriptions of what shape this might take. In response to the question about their everyday life, unlike Christian (and especially Protestant) respondents in previous studies, but like Buddhist responses, hardly anyone in the Muslim sample referred to their work.[6] More typical was the answer of Kaliq, a second-generation Muslim who prays at Ibad Allah. Salat is important, he says, "because you get beat up by what is going on in society, everybody struggles . . . You need a break from that or just talking to people, you hear a bunch of stressful stories, and you get frustrated in life." And so without the break provided by salat "you will blow up." Salat provides a pillow for you five times a day, he thinks. His work at the center exposes him to lots of relationship problems, and, he says, he needs a break from these. Nero feels a sense of urgency to his prayers, not to delay or put them off, "because," he says, "I want something beautiful to happen?" And what is this, our interviewer asked? "Well, it's to become closer to God, and to become a better human being." His prayers help him "feel more at ease . . . more calm, and that's a positive feeling to face the challenges of life."

6. This difference, in comparison to Christian respondents, is striking, since the protocols were basically unchanged.

In one sense it would seem that these life-giving practices provide an escape from everyday life; they do not appear to illumine that life. They offer comfort and motivation surely, but they also structure a religious life that stands apart from, even over against, the secular world. What about that other world outside the mosque? In fairness we recall these practices and the accompanying teachings are meant to order the whole of the Muslim's life, authorized as they are by the words of God himself, as given through the Prophet. And while very few made any comment on it, the notion of Shariah law implies that the will of Allah is meant to extend to the whole of life. But what does the Muslim do when she lives in a secular society whose laws do not necessarily reflect this divine will? Are the instructions of the Quran (and the Hadith) occluded by the reality of a state conceived as separate from religion? The answers of our respondents, and probably the limitations of the questions themselves, make it impossible for us to answer these questions, but such questions are critical for the practice of Islam in a religiously pluralistic society, and scholars are increasingly discussing them.[7]

Some respondents did make suggestions that provide partial answers to these questions. One possible approach might be provided by an important (and topical) application of Muslim faith to life in the world: the obligation for Muslim women to wear the hijab (which means headscarf but is loosely used to refer more generally to the veil). Unlike France there has been no general opposition to this practice on the part of U.S. culture (though some women in our sample reported being bothered by people staring at them). What does the practice mean to Muslim women? Shehla, the wife of one of the imams in Mission Viejo, thinks wearing a scarf is essential. The Hijab strengthens her Muslim identity she says, "because it's an obligation . . . If you see a Muslim . . . [and] she's not wearing the hijab, it doesn't mean it's an option. She's not following. It doesn't mean she's . . . a bad Muslim, but everybody has his weaknesses, so she's not following that part, but maybe she's following in other parts." She admits that she's the only one wearing in her home—neither her mother nor her sister are

7. The question of whether one can live as a Muslim in a non-Muslim territory has occupied jurists for centuries. Formerly Muslims were encouraged to move to Muslim dominated areas, but recently scholars allow them to live outside the Dar al-Islam (House of Islam) provided they can fulfill their religious obligations. (Rida, a prominent scholar, even argues that it would be a "sin" to bind oneself by Sharia in non-Muslim areas since this would lead to dependence and powerlessness, and thus contradict the aim of Sharia, which is the welfare of the people.) See Abou El Fadl, "Striking a Balance."

covering. "Maybe it's a matter of time, a matter of guidance." Shehla expects "that Allah will guide them one day."

Lela thinks following the obligation for women to cover up is important because it reminds you that "being a Muslim affects everything you do," including the way you dress. When she still lived in London just after 7/7, she started covering up, and at first her father was totally against it (though he has since changed his mind). People thought that she was being forced to cover up by her husband or parents. But, she insists, "It was not like that at all. In fact when I started covering . . . people [asked me] have you met a man? . . . And I was like no, no, it's just for me. It's a very . . . personal thing. It's between you and God; you know you can't do it for someone else." Lela's case is significant because she is able to describe the way Islam is personal but not private. It is not simply about something that is inside oneself, she argues, "it affects everything, everything—the way I interact with my husband, and the way, you know, I am at work, and with my family." Even when people around don't understand what she does, she insists: I say to them "peace be upon you."

Islamic Center of Southern California

Lela's sense of her own agency supports the argument of Saba Mahmood in her study of the Women's Mosque movement in Cairo. Outside observers, especially secular feminists, are likely to understand the obligation to wear headscarves as a social imposition, something that impedes the freedom (and agency) of these women. To the contrary, Mahmood says, these women see such practices as "potentialities, the 'scaffolding' if you will, through which the self is realized."[8] They find these practices enhance rather than limit their agency. The testimony of these women also demonstrates the way Islam provides an orientation that provides moral guidance on the one hand, and satisfies and gives life on the other. But notice too that it is the physical appropriation of this practice—the performance, in their everyday lives, that brings meaning to these women.

A further answer to the apparent split between religious practice and everyday life is provided by the case of Pui Lan, a graphic artist who prays at OCIF. She and her husband were frustrated because they could not find any Islamic art that was modern in style. So she began to create and select traditional Muslim designs and calligraphy done in a modern style. Soon friends commented on this and she realized this was a business opportunity. Now she sells these on her website and at various Muslim conferences around the country. What she likes best about her work is its connection to her faith. As she noted: "This is related to my religion. I can work, work religiously all the time, with something complementing my religion, and as what I like. I like making art. I like design. That's how it started."

Pui Lan, though motivated by wanting to see Islamic art, did not start her business to *express* her religion, but she has nevertheless taken her faith into the business world. Her products after all are Muslim designs and Quranic calligraphy. As she says later in the interview she sees this as a form of "outreach." But Pui Lan's art is not a form of witness in a secular sphere, such as a Christian artist might undertake, it is rather an extension of her practices of faith—a shariah-like attempt to remake the world in the image of God's will.

The Mosque and the Visibility of Community

If the time of Muslims is structured by salat, one might say their sense of place is oriented by the space of the mosque. When asked what he likes best about going to the King Fahad Mosque, Tanim answered: "It's the house of God, so you feel protected, you know, you feel the presence, because there's a lot of angels in the house of God . . . Because it is the house of God and because it is solely . . . to pray, you feel like it is very enhanced. It's the

8. Mahmood, *Politics of Piety*, 148.

house of God, right? So you feel very protected and pure." He especially likes the community aspect, where he can catch up with his friends, learn about community issues, or study theological subjects. Though he thinks King Fahad is a beautiful mosque—he went to great lengths describing its beauty—this "does not strengthen" him. In fact he claims he does not feel a strong connection to any particular mosque. It is more about the praying, he says, than the aesthetics. Because for him the core of Islam is moral—remember he confessed earlier that praying helps him control his tendency to lie. Tanim is typical of many who enjoy the beauty of the calligraphy, the colors of the decorations, but insist all this plays no role in their prayers. But, also like others, when asked what image he connects with his present experience, he immediately says "the mosque." Visually the mosque first comes to his mind, he says, and then he thinks of the Quran and calligraphy. And when he reflects on when he feels closest to God, he answers "when we're praying in congregation, men are standing next to one another, feet by feet touching, creating rows and rows upon rows, shoulder to shoulder . . . and the way we all bow, we all simultaneously bow down and move up . . . I feel a sense of unity . . . pure brotherhood." So the physical connection with the community—the Umma, becomes a strong image for him. And for him this "image" takes very definite visual forms. He goes on to describe the image of millions of the faithful circling the Kabah in Mecca (though he has not himself gone on the Hajj—the pilgrimage to Mecca—he has seen pictures), and points out that all mosques are oriented toward that one place. He thinks in fact there's a light (nur) beaming directly from that holy place into every mosque, "there's a sense of the visual that I see" in this connection, especially during the monthlong fast of Ramadan. Tanim looks up and reads for us a passage from the Quran, which says "God is the light of the heavens and the earth," and, Tanim says, God gives his light to guide us, to sculpt our lives.

Tanim's confession is not unusual. While disavowing any aesthetic attraction in praying, he can go on to describe a quite elaborate aesthetics of worship that connects him to the mosque—the calligraphy of Quranic verses, the visual rows of men praying, the light he sees emanating from the Kabah, and so on. But this all centers on the space of the mosque and on the pattern of practices that give life to that space. Like many, Tanim believes the space of the mosque is a safe place—a place of peace. Naim Shaw thinks the very structure of the place speaks of peace—it is for him, "the home of the soul." Edina of King Fahad Mosque likes the privacy of the space, its serenity, and cleanliness. It is a place where she can feel safe, where her modesty is preserved: "No one is looking at me." She finds the way this space and its prayers structures her life "a beautiful thing."

Masjid Ibad Allah

What is interesting to me is the way, for many, a strong rejection of the role of imagery in prayers can seem perfectly consistent with an aesthetic shaped by the visual practices of praying, and especially the light, shape, and space of the mosque. When thinking about Muslim worship one might be tempted to say that the space of the mosque is a place to listen and hear, but not to see. And in fact many did speak about trying to focus their minds and not let their eyes wander and so on. But such a conclusion would be overly simplistic. For the experience of worship for these worshipers is from start to finish a visual one as well as an oral one. Rather, one ought to say that all the images and practices of Islam, both oral and visual, are ordered and integrated into their experience in the mosque. Nero still remembers the first time he visited a mosque in Egypt. "That was a very old, grand mosque, so when I entered the place, the prayer area, I really did feel something very powerful. There were all these men praying here, and it was a huge place, and something hit me very, very deeply. Of course it was visual, because I had no understanding of anything else in regards to Islam . . . but the visual imagery was very powerful . . . This huge, vast empty place . . . just the open space, the openness of the space, I think, that's what really hit me."

The space of the mosque gives Muslims an integrated sense of place in several senses. First of all, as we have seen, the space itself is physically oriented toward Islam's most sacred place: the Kabah in Mecca. The lines of the architecture, the placement of the mihrab (or empty niche speaking of presence of the invisible God), and even the design of the carpet, serve to direct the worshiper toward Mecca. Secondly the mosque provides the space in which the Quran can be seen and heard, where it is written on the walls, where it is recited and studied. Moreover in the patterned prayers of the faithful these oral and visual aspects are integrated. As Dardess and Rosenthal note, the scale and size of the space is not enough in themselves to express God's greatness. Bigness can be oppressive, they point out. Rather "what is required is a way of working with large forms so that they become symbols of what is not merely great but *akbar,* 'that which is great beyond all measure of greatness.'"[9] This requires, for Mulsims, an integration of spatial and ritual aspects of worship.

So when Muslims are asked about the place of symbols and images in their religious experience, it is not surprising that they frequently refer to the mosque as the place where all these come together. When asked this question, Farhana responded that she doesn't really connect her religious experience to images or symbols. But she does connect it "mostly to mosques, but that's architectural, but that's probably because of the kind of interaction I have with community . . . I understand the Muslim community as . . . very mosque focused."

Moreover the experience of Muslims with their mosque is often a deeply aesthetic one. This too is unsurprising when one reflects that, in the mosque, the call to prayer and recitation of the Quran are sung, the calligraphy on the walls is fluid and graceful, and the space of the mosque is peaceful and welcoming—and frequently architecturally rich. When asked what role the space of the mosque played in their prayers, respondents, even while rejecting any role for images, made frequent reference to the beauty of the place. Mufti noted: "There are no images or anything distracting on

9. Dardess and Rosenthal, *Reclaiming Beauty for the Good of the World,* 77.

the walls, other than the Quran . . . there's a blank space which is, I think important as well when engaging in prayer. The carpets are all uniform color, the walls are all uniform color with the exception of the verses of the Quran . . . So there is a beauty in having nothing there, that blank canvas creates an opportunity for you to focus on what you are saying in prayer." Shahed, though she is a painter, likes the fact that the walls are blank, because then she says, "you get to paint your own picture in your head of how [you] want to see things . . . it doesn't limit your creativity . . . [it] makes you creative as to how you think God is, how you think the prophets look."

Space at Imam Center

What is striking, in a supposedly aniconic faith, is the recurrent reference to the visual elements of the mosque that draw and attract, and to the deep emotional connection worshipers feel with this space. Lela loves the King Fahad Mosque, especially the chandelier and the dome. "It feels like there's a lot of light and you can walk round there . . . and I always see men praying and things, so it's just really beautiful. It's very quiet . . . the architecture is really peaceful, so it just kind of really settles you . . . this is your time to be with God." Edina agrees with this assessment of the visual environment. She says, "Certain colors seem to be common in Islamic architecture.

And there's a beauty [in] the pillars, the separations, the way a mosque is developed. I think those are all symbols of [what] draws us to our mosque."

Beyond the physical shape of the mosque, one can argue that the very human patterning of prayer has an aesthetic quality to it. Though human images are forbidden in the mosque, the actual shape of worshipers, row upon row, bowing in perfect order, is in fact a striking "image" that arrests the imagination. One can even say that this constitutes a living image that Muslims (and often outsiders) find deeply moving. For this figure portrays better than any teaching the actual oneness that characterizes the Umma— the community of Islam. Gordon, the African American from Iowa, thinks this image reflects the order that comes with Islam. When asked what draws his eyes during prayer, he answered: "The lines on the floor." He explained: "We are all one group of people, so we all have one line that we pray on, one direction that we face, we all have one God that we pray to and we are all one community." When it's time to pray, he says, everyone takes their place in the line and "that's an aspect of the beauty of everything in general." Saif thinks that even the pattern on the carpet reinforces this sense of order and direction. "It has a pattern . . . to point out the direction of Mecca, which is the direction that all Muslims face during prayer." Even the position of the prayer leader, standing in front by the mihrab, orders the congregation. The structure and order defines a particular aesthetic, and the typical response to this conjunction of the spacious open feel of the mosque, the order of the praying worshipers, and the often moving recitation and chanting is as strongly aesthetic as it is religious—in fact, for many, these cannot be separated.

In questions relating to art and beauty I was struck by how often re-spondents referred to architecture as important to them. When one thinks of Muslim practices as connecting one to God, structuring one's life, and the centrality of the mosque, this is not surprising—architecture structures space in ways that move people in one direction or another. Farhana kept coming back to "the architecture thing" when talking about the way the mosque is to encourage a sense of openness. Lela, who grew up in London but became committed to her ancestral Muslim faith after visiting Iran, admitted that architecture is her thing. "I think having good architecture, it draws people to whatever it is, so you just tend to be . . . drawn to it."

King Fahad Mosque

Suhaib from OCIF who just graduated with a degree in architecture makes explicit the connection between architecture, art, and the mosque. For his senior project he designed a contemporary mosque, one that was influenced in part by the new Our Lady of Angels Catholic Cathedral in downtown Los Angeles. He likes the fact the modernism has done away with ornamentation. In his design, which is a square prayer room with glass walls, there is no decoration. As he put it, the structure itself serves as the only "ornament." One enters the space by walking down, which portrays the humbling of oneself before God. Since prayer is the center of one's life, the prayer room stands at the center of his design, with spaces for classes, a farmer's market, and a gym ranged around this. Suhaib is typical of many when he says he can pray anywhere, and that he prefers environments that are free of distraction. Yet the care he has given to his design for a mosque indicates that the place where one prays, and the space it contains, matter a great deal.

Shahed from Sri Lanka prays in the Islamic Center (ICSCA) and is a painter herself. She insisted there is no disconnect between art and Islam because, she thinks, "there is a very strong connection to God in art." Whether in the beauty of nature or reading the Quran or praying, "I feel that's kind of my own approach to how I . . . practice my art, of how I do that. I felt those same connects [sic]." These connections were first awakened during an early trip to Saudi Arabia and to Mecca. "I think just being at the mosque and seeing [religious imagery] everywhere, in the architecture. I think that architecture is probably what really exposed me to it . . . It wasn't that I was looking at it as art. It was architecture first and its incorporation of calligraphy or Islamic art or the geometric configuration that are used in Islamic architecture." She was young when she first saw this, but it made a lasting impression on her. One might say that just as visual art is derived in a general sense from calligraphy and from the actual Arabic words of God, so the arts and calligraphy are parasitic on architecture. For the architecture of the mosque structures the space, and orients believers in the direction of the Kabah in Mecca, just as the religious practices—the ablutions, prayers, and prostrations structure the lives of Muslims.

Conclusion: Spiritual Architecture—The Struggle to Orient One's Life

In the words of these respondents we have frequently heard reference to orientation and to structure, especially in the way the practices orient one toward God, and the space of the mosque is structured to encourage this sense of oneness. To these we might add a further related idea that of "building." Abdul, who prays at Ibad Allah, thinks the dynamics of a mosque attracts a person (he mentions the Taj Mahal and the Alhambra); this "enhances a person's thinking to please their Lord." He goes on to note that those who are attracted by the sound of the Quran are moved to "express our love of life by putting it into something beautiful to please the Creator, because [the Quran] said that if you build a house on earth to worship the Creator, he will build a house for you in paradise, so of course you're going to put together a beautiful house that's even beyond your imagination. So . . . you will see beautiful things that come out [of] your heart." The appropriate response to listening to the Quran, if Abdul is right, is the process of building a beautiful life for God. The immediate sense of this is building the space where one will worship, which is meant to be an image of paradise, an enclosed garden with the fountain in the middle. But, by extension, Abdul surely is referring to structuring one's life, the patient sculpting of oneself into a beautiful vessel. The five pillars—itself an architectural term—become the means to this construction. We noted earlier the Christian concern that these practices might obscure a heartfelt faith in God. This worry would surely puzzle a Muslim believer, for the prayers and the ablutions are the place where this faith is constructed.

This process of construction involves personal effort, what Muslims call jihad, but it is always a corporate project. There is a deep awareness of belonging to a worldwide brotherhood all united and oriented in a single direction—a reality visible at every mosque and during every ritual prayer. Jamal of the Iman Center pointed to a picture of a door on the wall when he was being interviewed. It is, he said, "the door of the Kabah. They say it looks like heaven's door also." Why is that important? "It's the most important symbolism . . . to just make the people [face] in one direction, that's probably the only symbol that we have. And that is not to worship that place, it is only to concentrate everybody in one direction, with . . . one aim." Aasif of Idad Allah thinks the role of the masjid (mosque) is to move one to this oneness "that should be instilled in the whole universe, because the universe . . . should work together as one to worship God . . . So the focus, the oneness of people during salat and their attempt to become one with one another, to become clean with one another, to interact in a positive [way] toward one another is to me best felt inside of these masjids."

All of this suggests that a possible guiding image of the Muslim aesthetic might be termed the practice of a *spiritual architecture*. Time and again respondents made reference to architecture as their preferred art or as summing up the role that art and aesthetics played in their devotion. For architecture, in the sense I intend it, does not simply create a space, but sets in motion a dynamic that connects people to God, to each other, and, at the moment of prostration, to the earth. Mufti describes this master image when at the end of his interview he was asked whether there was anything else about his faith he wanted to say. This is what he said: "Again, I think architecture is probably the most important aspect of Islamic art to me because it is utilized regularly by worshipers for connecting to God, and that space that is created is profound, to enable that or to facilitate that event . . . that group prayer, that collective yet individual connection to God."

Jihad took this image a step further. Though you will remember he was generally suspicious of images, he was eager to describe the pattern of arches and columns on the carpet in the men's prayer room of his Orange

County mosque. He thinks that when the men line up on this carpet to pray they "become their own architecture." This symbolism is critical he thinks; he's proud of it!

The practices of Islam then represent the spiritual architecture of building one's life, struggling to keep the proper orientation—symbolically toward the most sacred place in Mecca, and in everyday life working to be connected to God and to one another. Laboring to structure one's days according to this orientation. Building one's life, stone upon stone, one prayer at a time.

Women praying at Ibad Allah

Christians speak often about spiritual formation and the practices that promote this—prayer, the study of Scripture, and the fellowship they find with other Christians. But interestingly the Muslim practices of prayer in the mosque are formational in a way unlike Christian worship services. Muslim worshipers speak of prayers as disciplining, giving peace, and structuring their lives. Very few Christians (at least of the Protestant variety) would describe their Sunday worship in terms of order or discipline. More likely they would speak of the "take away" from these services, the lessons and insights they provide for their life in the world. Like the Sufi responses we described, Christians often worry that an overemphasis on ritual and practice can detract from the meaning they are supposed to carry. Most Muslim respondents that we have heard would surely find this concern odd. How can the performance of these practices, which have over time become so formative and enriching, be considered dispensable? For the Muslims of our sample, the satisfaction is intrinsic to the practices themselves; it does not reside in the meaning or application of these to their everyday lives. These differences are not trivial and they will be central to our discussion of aesthetic difference in the conclusion.

I began this chapter reflecting on the difference between the Christian symbolism of Christ's presence in worship and that of the Prophet Muhammad, and it might be appropriate to end there as well. When Christian worshipers stand to hear the reading of the Gospel, they are honoring Christ surely, but in an important sense they are also acknowledging his physical absence. As they repeat each week, "Christ has died, Christ is risen, Christ will come again," they acknowledge that Christ's presence is spiritual—that is mediated by the Spirit, and they await his bodily return at the end of history. By contrast, when Muslim worshipers hear the words of the Quran, or when they see and touch the pages of Arabic script, they are celebrating a presence. The Quran is the physical and visible presence of God in a way that Scripture, however inspired, cannot be. This entails special practices of prayer and recitation but also a particular aesthetic of patterns, arabesque, and symmetry—developed as these are into various schools of calligraphy. This spiritual geometry gives the space of the mosque its special dynamic, as Naim Shaw puts it, as the house of the soul.

But the Gospel reading and the narrative it recounts give Christian worship its unique energy, opening a path, Christians believe, that leads to death and resurrection. One might even say that Christians feel they are themselves called to be the physical presence of Christ in the world. The standing and the reading are means to this end but with this difference: whatever aesthetic purpose they serve is subordinated to the meaning of the reading. Again I am made aware of the focus on the narrative and events of

Christ's life, which lends Christian worship a different focus and a distinct dynamic. For Muslims the events of the life of Muhammad are important and they are recalled especially during the monthlong fast of Ramadan. But they do not constitute the dynamic of Muslim worship in the way Christ's biography does for Christians. When in some Christian churches the pastor kisses the Gospel before reading it, he or she is not acknowledging the presence of God so much as celebrating the life recounted there, and its spiritual power. This proposes a different impulse and different possibilities for beauty. These differences we will explore further in the conclusion.

Conclusion: Aesthetic and Devotional Trajectories

Introduction: In Search of Living Images

In our research across four major religious traditions, it has become clear that art objects, ritual practice, and background beliefs are grounded in communities and integrated over time into typical patterns. Respondents, who have come to feel at home in one or another of these traditions often spoke warmly about these configurations. In one, art objects—or what Orthodox Christians call icons—may be more prominent; in another ritual or meditative practices come to the fore; and in another background beliefs become regulative both of objects and practice. In this conclusion I will make a preliminary attempt to describe and assess these differences. Though the focus is clearly on the findings from Buddhist and Muslim interviews, the Christian perspective of the researchers, and their previous research, has been acknowledged and appropriated to further the discussion. The geographic and theological location of both the sample and the researchers, which I described in the preface, is a limitation, but by framing this as a conversation among adherents in a specific setting I have attempted to make this into an advantage. These brief comments are offered finally as suggestive of directions interfaith conversation, and future research, might profitably take.

The cumulative voices of our respondents suggest that from the standpoint of lay members, distinctive patterns of practice, images, and beliefs are always embodied in a holistic way. Most of the time respondents, from each religious tradition, tended to speak of the various elements in relation to each other. In a previous study I have referred to such patterns of practice and objects as "complex images."[1] By this I intended to underline not only the close relationship that exists between practices and objects but

1. Dyrness, *Senses of the Soul*, 132.

the affective meaning these complexes have for believers. The elements that we focus on, whether they are visual images or ritual practices, do not function by themselves but interact in complex interrelationship. To use David Morgan's terms, we want to understand not just what these practices mean but what, together, they *do* in worshipers' lives. In our Christian study, we found that images or art artifacts that impact believers spiritually can be appreciated on their own terms, but more often they make up a complex of visual and ritual items: a congregant carrying in the cross during Lent, a priest raising the Host, even the congregation lifting their hands during a song, all these and many others can serve as "complex images" that impact worshipers in multiple ways.

This study confirmed that such complex images are also to be found in Buddhist and Muslim religious practice. With a primary focus on these traditions, in this chapter I want to consider the similarities and differences between various complex images. But I want also to expand on this idea and describe them in terms of what I will call *living images*. I have borrowed the term from a recent study of John Calvin by Randall Zachman.[2] Calvin distinguished between dead images, which humans create in a futile attempt to bring God down from heaven, and living images, which God alone can create. For Calvin, Zachman says, living images are transformative for the person contemplating them. They have both analogical and anagogical relation to the reality they represent, and they "offer" or present to the viewer (or hearer since these were mostly communicated through preaching) the reality being referred to—whether this be an element of creation, an event of Israel or the church's history, or a (sacramental) setting forth of Christ in preaching or the Eucharist. The particular Christian perspective developed by Calvin need not detain us here—though it will be relevant when we describe our Christian framework—but the notion of living images seems to me a felicitous way to describe the particular symbolic patterns that religious traditions display.

Living images, as I will use the term, are those patterns of practice and images that "come alive" for adherents in the enacted performance of their tradition. It is the experience of peace that meditation brings for Buddhists or the felt connection with God during prostration for Muslims. That is, the factors that move these believers result not simply from what practices or

---

2. Zachman, *Image and Word in the Theology of John Calvin*, 7–8. Calvin wanted to contrast living images offered in God's revelation with "dead" images, that is, the physical images and altarpieces found in the Catholic churches made by humans.

beliefs might be considered normative for a given faith, but from the actual appropriation of these by people in the course of their worship or meditation—these are images that are put into play by performance. But living images are alive in a second sense. They "come alive" in the performance, but they also, at the same time, are "life-giving," in that people report they are transformed or enriched in some way by them. This focus on holistic and life-giving practice seems to me to be a fruitful component in interfaith conversations—one that is often missing. Many discussions, especially when they are based on sacred texts or other written material, begin with assumptions about what is normative in the traditions—they compare what amounts to normative or ideal types. This not only risks marginalizing the lay, or nonprofessional perspectives, but, what is worse, can too easily result in comparing my ideal image with your (sometimes) confused reality.

Two further reminders are necessary before we move to a discussion of the religious traditions themselves. My colleagues and I have chosen to use the methodology of the study of visual or sensory culture as a way into religious traditions—something that I briefly defended in the introduction. We are interested in learning how visual elements—space, ritual practice, and various religious artifacts have the power to arrest the mind, move the emotions, and provide places where "belief happens."[3] We use this methodology not to *reduce* religious practice to these elements, but to *broaden* our understanding of faith traditions in order to describe more fully these religious imaginations. This broadened perspective allows us to study embodied behavior and responses in space and time as religiously significant. This does not diminish the importance of sacred texts but seeks to understand the ways these are internalized and performed.

But second, recall that we are alert to the *aesthetics* of religious practice. Our reflections on the traditions we studied enable us to elaborate this dimension of religious practice a bit further here. I have been helped by the image of "interlacing" as a description of the relation between art and religion. The notion, as developed by Cecilia González-Andrieu, takes "seriously the faith experience of the communities producing and receiving the art," and at the same time questions more abstract methodologies.[4] Because of this experiential focus, she notes, a richness is already present in the materials studied. She pictures the interlacing of the religious and the aesthetic as a "braid." Here is how she describes this: "As we picture a braid,

3. Morgan, *The Sacred Gaze*, 8.
4. Gonzalez-Andrieu, *Bridge to Wonder*, 84.

it is possible to appreciate that the uniqueness of each thread is precisely what contributes to the dynamism and complexity of the multistranded rope, and it is the action of intricate weaving that makes this possible."[5] It seems to me her image has special application to the way religious communities develop patterns of practice. In our terminology "living images" are the result of the interlacing of meaning, ritual, and visual surface into a whole that is, in a significant way, aesthetic. Elements of religious practice, we have found, as they are combined in the experience of prayer or meditation, have visual (or aural) power to arrest the mind and move the emotions. This power is, in part, aesthetic in that these elements are interlaced—figured, in such a way, that when they are seen or heard they spark desire, elicit joy, or in some cases wonder and awe. Obviously this does not keep these experiences from being theologically (or in nontheistic traditions, metaphysically) significant, but suggests that this deeper reality is invariably mediated and charged aesthetically. It seems to me the notion of "living images" nicely captures these qualities.

If the aesthetics of worship results from the interlacing of various elements, the question arises as to which elements precisely contribute to this effect. We have spoken variously about visual, oral, and ritual elements and the way these, separately and together, impact believers during worship. We have referred to these as places and spaces where belief (or meaning) takes shape. In these concluding comments I would like to say more about these elements and their interrelationship in the traditions we are studying. To get at these differences I have been helped by Saba Mahmood's study of the women's mosque movement in Cairo, Egypt, to which I referred earlier.[6] The goal of these women of "being close to God," she discovered involved a complex disciplinary program in which virtues are developed and expressed in the performance of their religious duties. The intention to follow God entailed a prescribed sequence of gestures, words, and attitudes. These women, Mahmood argued, developed their sense of self in the performance of these practices. She summarizes this process by saying: "The *work* bodily practices perform in crafting a subject—rather than the *meanings* they signify—carries the analytic weight. In other words the 'how' of the practices is explored rather than their symbolic or hermeneutical value."[7]

---

5. Ibid., 88.

6. Mahmood, *Politics of Piety*, 122.

7. Ibid., (her emphasis).

I want to develop this fruitful notion by suggesting that religious traditions may be described, in part, by the relative weight they give to the work of embodied practices over against the meanings they signify. I want further to include, alongside bodily practices—or ritual and its meaning—visual cues and responses to images and the arrangement of space. During the course of our study then, three elements have emerged as critical to the formation and experience of complex images: cognitive and linguistic representations, ritual-embodied practices, and visual cues provided by objects and spatial arrangements.[8] Here I want to describe these various elements more fully.

The first of these, linguistic representation, refers to the role that verbal formulations—creeds, confessions, scriptures, play in religious practice. The second addresses the ritual practices that traditions have developed both to form and express religious emotions. The last, the visual and spatial cues—the special focus of our study—considers the role external visual factors play in ordering religious devotion. It might be argued that the second and third category are overlapping since both deal with sensory experience, but our reflection on the data led us to distinguish them: the second involves the active agency of the adherent, while the third addresses the (more passive) reception of visual (and other sensory) elements. The former is performed; the latter experienced. These factors, I argue, are "theory laden," that is, the inclination toward them is shaped by the disciplinary matrix of the tradition,[9] as this is mediated by the training the person has received.[10] They embody and express the deep structure of these faiths.

Specifically then I am interested in a three-sided relationship between and among beliefs, ritual, and visual (and oral) artifacts. It seems to me that in addition to comparing, say, similar rituals in various religious traditions, one has to also compare the relative weight that a particular ritual plays in a given tradition over against other elements. In Eastern Orthodox Christianity, for example, visual cues—icons and their use in the liturgy, are essential

8. In developing these elements I have been stimulated by the research of Tanya Luhrmann. See Luhrmann et al., "Absorption" 67, 68. She and her colleagues describe what they call interpretation (the cognitive/linguistic dimension), and practice (the subjective and psychological consequences of specific training, e.g., prayer). See her earlier article "Metakinesis," 518. She describes practice as "metakinesis"—the way emotional experience is carried within the body. See now the recent work, Luhrmann, *When God Talks Back*.

9. Cf. Asad, *Genealogies of Religion*, 55–79.

10. Luhrmann's research leads her to add what she calls personal "proclivity," that is "a talent for and willingness to respond to practice" ("Absorption," 67).

to the experience of prayer, and so the visual and symbolic elements come to the fore. Scholars have noted the way the visual images have carried the theological weight in this tradition.[11] Meanwhile in Islam, according to Mahmood, the performance all but supplants the symbolic meaning (though my study will lead me to nuance her claim later). To take another illustration, one might compare Buddhist meditation with what Christians call "centering prayer" and find great similarities. But the (very different) role these play in the two imaginations, and the balance they sustain with other elements, would belie such easy comparison. Both are religiously and personally important and bear a certain superficial resemblance. But the Christian assumes a specific interpretation of God's presence and seeks to join the self to this God, while the Buddhist practice seeks to eliminate the self ("anatta" or no-self). The difference lies not in the practice itself so much as the relationship this sustains to other factors. What became clear in listening to our respondents was not only the *presence* of such elements, whether there be three, four, or more of them, but the *relative weight* and value given to each of them in a given religious tradition. In the conclusion then I will focus on these elements and seek to describe the particular contour of interlacing that characterizes the traditions under consideration.

A Christian Aesthetics of Worship: Singing a New Song

While this study is not directly about a Christian aesthetics of worship, my comments throughout about a Christian response to various Muslim and Buddhist practices have suggested what such an aesthetic might be. So here it may be appropriate to fill out these suggestions, very briefly—something not done in my previous study, but stimulated by this comparative study. How do we understand a Christian imagination when it comes to worship? Catholic or Orthodox Christians bring their own suppositions to worship, so let me speak here about my own Protestant (and Reformed) understanding of worship. I have already referred to the creedal formula repeated in many liturgies: "Christ has died, Christ is risen, Christ will come again." In many ways this could serve as an abbreviated statement of what is called the gospel, or good news, that Christians believe Christ taught—that is the narrative of the biblical account centering on the life and work of Christ. Such linguistic representations are critical for Protestant Christians. They are on display in various ways in Protestant worship—whether in reciting a

11. See Paul Evdokimov, *The Art of the Icon: A Theology of Beauty.*

creed, reading Scripture, or in listening to a sermon. For this reason Protestants often answered the question about what is central in worship or what connects this to their everyday life, by referring to the sermon, or the teaching.[12] The pastor of Grace Brethren Church in Long Beach who we interviewed in our previous study articulated well this emphasis in worship: "There are a variety of elements that we do in [the service] to engage people in this overarching story that we really try to emphasize here. It's not the worship. It's the story that prompts the worship . . . and that's an . . . important distinction, because . . . I think that so much about these worship wars is that we're fighting about worship . . . We need to change the scope of the argument. That if we were about the story, [we would see] that it's really much larger than us, that worship is prompted by the story."

This means that for Protestants, all other (ritual and visual) elements must be oriented by this "story." Jose is a Filipino-American artist in one of the Protestant congregations we studied. He is happy to see people connect with art in the church, but when it comes to worship, what is important, he thinks, is the personal adoration of God. "The process of starting with praise and then . . . if the conditions are right [and] the Holy Spirit is there, with the talent of the worship leader [and] the ambiance, my frame of mind, of being able to really enter into worship and adoration. That's for me the goal, and sometimes that happens—it doesn't always happen." What sparks this, Jose implies, is the realization and appropriation of the meaning of the story.

But one question elicited an unexpected response. We asked Protestant worshipers: "At what point in the service are you moved to prayer, or experience the presence of God? What triggers this?" Of the thirty-nine responses, twenty-one mentioned some form of music. And of these only eight specifically mentioned the words—the lyrics—or put music in relation to the sermon. (Only two even mentioned the sermon as triggering prayer or closeness to God, and these mentioned it only in connection with music!) No other category had more than one or two responses, except communion (Eucharist) and nature, which had four each. This supports the argument that, though the story about what God has done in Christ is central to Protestant worship, in order for this to move the worshipers— for

12. This was also the conclusion of Susan Harding's study of fundamentalist belief. This focus led her to argue, that among these believers "[l]istening to the gospel enables you to experience belief, as it were, vicariously. But generative belief that indisputably transfigures you and your reality, belief that becomes you, comes only through speech: speaking is believing" (*The Book of Jerry Falwell*, 60).

it to become a living image—it had to take on aesthetic, or in this case a musical form.[13] As one woman said, when pressed about what it was about music she found so deeply moving: "The words," she said. Seeing what Christ has done for me "puts me down on my knees in gratefulness . . . how he is powerful and yet he loves me."

For these worshipers the experience of singing songs, especially when they reflect on the words, can be very moving. But notice that what facilitates this dynamic is loaded heavily on the side of meaning. To use Mahmood's terms, such linguistic representation is what carries the analytic weight. Practices such as baptism and Eucharist are important, but their importance is parasitic on the story—believers are buried and raised with Christ in baptism; they remember, represent, and share in the death of Christ in communion, and so on. Of course Catholics and Orthodox believers would understand this balance differently. It is helpful here to recall Edward Muir's account of medieval Christians being taught to adore and not to think—that is, in that period the practice itself carried the weight. Such practices, during that earlier period, sparked wonder and faith. At the Reformation linguistic representation and the thinking it sparked began to predominate, in some cases all but supplanting the experience of the sacrament. And so Reformers struggled to resolve the tension between the meaning and the experience of these practices.[14]

And Protestants still struggle with this. In many ways this tension has increased with the modern (post-Enlightenment) focus on personal faith and individual decision. Images and practices may move the emotions, but what should drive the response, they insist, is the meaning of Christ's life and death. It follows from this that in some cases Protestants consider practice, even the worship service itself, to be dispensable—nothing but a dead image. Sam (interestingly, a filmmaker) from a church in Orange County, put it this way: "The worship experience there . . . isn't exclusive to that moment, it is part of our week, it is part of something that we choose to participate in, but if it goes away we're all going to survive, we're all going to know Christ still and we're all going to be able to worship him apart from that if we have to." Though this is a typical Protestant attitude, it is hard to

---

13. This is consistent with a study done by Peter Marsden that shows that, surprisingly, Protestants are significantly more likely than either Catholics or Jews to say that art brings them closer to God, since in his study music was included in the arts (Marsden, "Religious Americans and the Arts in the 1990s," 66). I believe when the Protestants were asked about "art" they naturally (and perhaps primarily) thought about music!

14. See Muir, *Ritual in Early Modern Europe*, 172–79.

imagine a Buddhist saying this about meditation, or a Muslim about the ablution and prayers in the mosque!

The struggle over the role and place of ritual and images, does not keep Protestants from espousing their own particular aesthetic of worship, even if this is often unnoticed. After all there is still a visual culture, there is music and some kind of oral communication, and the forms these take invariably move worshipers in one way or another. How might such an aesthetic be described? What constitutes for Protestants a "living image" in worship? Though put in various ways many Protestant respondents would agree with Carol Anderson, formerly the rector of All Saints Church in Beverly Hills, when she describes the goal of the visual and ritual elements as "simplicity and elegance." All the "machinations," she thinks, need to be "orchestrated in a strange way for all of us to get out of the way." Bad worship, she thinks, is really "inattentiveness that takes your mind off the things you should be concentrating on, which is God or God's word . . . whether its musical or visual or aesthetic . . . All of those are secondary to how you begin processing each of those and how your own heart is drawn into communion with God." When done well, these environmental elements, Carol thinks, "get out of the way and allow worshipers to experience God."

Simplicity, clarity, absence of clutter, or distraction—these all characterize a Protestant aesthetic of worship. For the mind should be directed to focus on God, and it is the announcement of God's word in the sermon, or even better in some form of music, that best allows the mind and heart to feel God's presence. In a fascinating way, these words resonate with similar responses from both Buddhist and Muslim respondents, both of which feature practices that direct the mind. But there is this central difference: the Protestant aesthetic of worship, whatever its visual and symbolic shape, necessarily appropriates the story, which worshipers, in their turn, are to live out in their everyday life.[15] With this most Protestants would agree, but what (visual or ritual) shape this ought to take, or whether it needs any visual shape at all, involves a tension that remains unresolved.

Let me then propose that the living image characteristic of the Protestant imagination might well be the *new song*, that believers sing in worship. It is significant that singing appeared as central to the responses about what moved them most deeply, especially when the protocol had no questions

15. And Christians believe that, like the message of the Quran, one cannot discover the biblical story on one's own—God had to reveal it to us. This Christian conviction, often misunderstood (or overlooked) by outsiders, accounts for the fact that Christians, like Muslims, see witness and mission as central religious practices.

specifically about music. While we cannot develop this further here, this focus on singing fits historically with the development of Protestant worship, from singing the Psalter in Calvin's Geneva, through the hymns of the evangelical awakenings, to the praise choruses of contemporary evangelical worship. Singing then is a useful trope for describing the aesthetics of Protestant worship. Life-giving worship encourages Protestants to shape the events of their life into a melody that they believe offers praise to God.

Buddhist Aesthetics: Chanting One's Life

Meditating at the Bodhi Path Sangha

Buddhism, according to Titus Burckhardt, has liquefied Hindu cosmic mythology and "turned it into images of states of the soul."[16] This focus on shaping states of the soul through various practices of meditation was consistent among our respondents. The image that emerged, I argued in an earlier chapter, is to see these mental disciplines as chanting—a chanting that absorbs differences into itself and, working with these, harmonizes them. Meditation in its various forms, respondents report, recognizes one's fundamental ignorance, and awakens one to the way things are, producing a mindful awareness that leads to equanimity. Buddhist practice is chanting

16. Burckhardt, *Sacred Art*, 163.

one's life. Life shaped in this way, our respondents report, can be seen as a harmonious whole. Chanting of course is a diverse practice of Buddhism that helps to direct the mind in various and specific ways. There is chanting that follows a particular Sanskrit text (also called reciting); there is chanting that repeats specific words or phrases; and of course there is meditation without any sound at all. But here I am appropriating chanting as a trope for Buddhist aesthetics; I am proposing that the mindful equanimity that is the goal of the enlightened mind can be captured as a life that is en-chanted.

In the earlier discussion I noted the tension between seeking a life lived in equanimity and the goal of decentering oneself via meditation so that life can be lived with compassion—the one focuses on release from samsara (the world of illusion), the other seeks to live compassionately in that world. I noticed at the time a similar tension exists in Christianity between a life lived in and for God, via prayer and meditation, and a life lived out in the world. I want to return here to this tension, or rather, to these different tensions. My goal is to explore how these traditions, at least with the evidence we have before us, deal differently with these tensions.

In order to understand this more closely let me start with the response of the Christian woman quoted above, let's call her Beth, to the words in the music that focused on what Christ did for her; this, she said, "put her down on her knees" in worship. By contrast remember the confession of Kim (previously an evangelical Christian) who was deeply moved by his bodhisattva vows, which he described as "living my life for others." We recall he felt being a dad helped him understand that "my life is no longer mine, it is theirs"—that it belongs to his children. This gives him great joy. "Living my life to help others . . . (he searches for the right word) . . . what more is there?" These responses clearly put before us a similarity and a difference that I want to explore.

On the surface it might seem that these two are not comparable; they are speaking about two very different, even incommensurate realities—the Christian relating her affective response to the work of Christ, the other the (equally emotional) response to bodhisattva vows he made. Mark Heim, however, in the paper we cited in the introduction, has recognized a certain family resemblance between the "dynamics" of the Christian view of "atonement"—that is what Christ's death does for the Christian and the bodhisattva vows.[17] His method is especially congenial to ours in that he expresses interest not so much in what Buddhists mean by the bodhisattva, and we might add, what Christians mean by the atonement, but the *way*

17. Heim, "Sharing Tensions," 7.

they go about answering these questions—as we have put it, we want to focus not so much on what is believed but *how* belief is expressed and enacted. While considering the similarities and differences, Heim underlines a significant point of comparison that is relevant to our discussion. He notes the bodhisattva ideal and the Christian view of atonement both express and resolve certain basic tensions in their respective traditions. There is much that Christians can learn by comparing Buddhist ideas of conventional and ultimate truth, with Christ's historical death and its universal application. But, I would argue, there is this difference: The bodhisattva ideal specifies primarily a spiritual practice; the atonement primarily refers to an historical event to which the believer is called to respond. The one specifies a ritual practice; the other articulates (and celebrates) meaning through a particular linguistic construal of an event. And so when confronted with the Buddhist focus, Heim finds himself asking of the atonement: what *social practices* are necessarily entailed in the work of Christ on the cross?

Christian responses, like that of Beth, characteristically focus on the desire to appropriate this event in their lives, as they typically say, to make it "real." The following response of Jose, a Filipino-American artist in a South Orange County megachurch, is representative of many. In response to the question of when in the service he is moved to prayer or feels the presence of God, he responded: "It's usually at a point where the worship becomes personal. For some reason I can identify personally with . . . what Christ went through for me personally. When I can get to that point of making it [real], I can relate to it and make it a personal experience that's usually the key." Protestant worshipers find experiences like this, which happen, we recall, most frequently in connection with music, transformative —they become "living images" for them.

But however transformative, such experiences are primarily about appropriating meaning, rather than stipulating some specific practice. Of course Christians all testify that the ultimate purpose of such experiences is to reorder their lives in ways consistent with Christ's life (and his death). As we noted, even the sacraments provide opportunity for believers to share in the life of Christ, to be conformed to his image. And the Christ story that orients Protestants in worship continues outside the service of worship—believers take the story with them into their week, and this can suggest an aesthetic than resonates with that of Buddhist respondents. Virginia Smith helps plan worship services in a Pentecostal church in the Eagle Rock district of L.A. She believes that God does not simply "let you live your life" but that he forms you through what you enjoy—including especially the fine music program of her church. When you walk out the door you are struck with what God has made, you are drawn, she says, to what is beautiful. "You know just that pure excitement of being able to enjoy something that is beautiful and is just a blessing . . . It also makes you feel embraced and welcomed and loved." These effects are gifts to be enjoyed surely, but from these testimonies, it appears they are not the stuff of faith; they are the fruit and not the tree. The tree is the story, which alone produces these effects.[18]

But how exactly does the tree yield the fruit that Christians look for? This raises complex theological questions that we cannot fully address here, but we can, with Mark Heim, suggest ways that Christians might learn here from the Buddhist focus on spiritual practice. He proposes that just as the bodhisattva practice changes the objective environment in which suffering is addressed, so Christ's work might be considered as a field of merit that can be actualized in various acts of Christian devotion. In this sense the cross can be understood as a social event. Just as Christ's intervention into my relationship with God can affect me (and others), so my forgiveness of another can affect a third person and so on.[19]

Heim's comparative discussion I find illuminating on several levels. But this learning takes place notwithstanding the continuing differences in Buddhist and Christian imagination and practice; In fact, I would argue, the learning takes place *only* when this difference is acknowledged and appropriated. Buddhists consistently say that they do not "use" external images in the way Christians use the account of Christ's death. In fact the question about what point they "feel most deeply moved" in their meditation simply made no sense to many of them. Off the record some of them expressed their confusion to our researchers and insisted that one "does not go deeper" in meditation. This is not to say that meditation does not change a person over time—"bottom line, it changes the brain" one of them said—or that masters who have spent their life meditating are not formed by the practice, but it is the *practice* that is cultivated not the affective or emotional depth. As Mei at Hsi Lai Temple put it, "I don't think of image. I meditate on my breathing and I get to a very peaceful place." (She is the one, we recall, who insisted "we don't have to go through Jesus or anybody;" we have to correct it from within.) Diane was raised a Protestant

18. I am well aware of the theological differences between, say, Lutherans and Reformed Protestants on this point, but I am describing here the broad commonality at the level of vernacular faith that was evident among our Protestant respondents.

19. Heim, "Sharing Tensions," 31. Cf. 29–33.

and experienced at Hsi Lai a transition when she learned from Buddhism to "let things happen as they come and try to work more on myself." Now she doesn't seek "answers" as concretely as she did before (notice that when she became Buddhist linguistic meaning came to carry very little analytic weight for her), rather she is trying to see how what she does affects others and her surroundings. "I . . . guess I'm the keeper of my own soul . . . generally we don't use the word soul, but I'm responsible for myself. I felt I like that sense of accountability . . . I get that more from within myself." Her chanting, her prostrations, help her let things go, to be at peace. They are for her "living images." The image of chanting, I think, helps us see that meditating (in the sangha) and letting things go (out in the world) are not separate activities. The latter is not the application of the former, they are part of an integrated whole—a chanted life.

Chanting and meditation directly cultivate a central aim of Buddhist life: detachment. Interestingly, detachment is also a Christian norm. Christ famously urged his disciples "not to worry about your life, what you will eat or what you will drink, or about your body, what you will wear. Is not life more than food and the body more than clothing?"(Matt 6:25). But, unlike Buddhism, this norm is not embodied and nurtured by any particular worship practice.[20]

At the Hsi Lai Temple, a pamphlet was available for visitors on "The Buddhist Perspective on Compassion." There the Venerable Master Hsing Yun describes bodhisattva's activated and awakened state in these terms: "Upon the seeing the suffering experienced by all beings, if a bodhisattva does not feel compassion, or aspire to reach Buddhahood and relieve all beings from suffering, then the journey to the Bodhi Path cannot be complete. Therefore compassion is the prerequisite for Buddhahood to a bodhisattva."[21]

Compassion, defined as "service offered out of selflessness and wisdom," is here conceived as a practice that is the essence of the bodhisattva nature. Notice that Kim experienced his bodhisattva vow as a "living image" because it awakened him to his call, as he put it, to "live his live for others." Val is moved by meditating with the sangha at Against the Stream—"it's very powerful to meditate with others," she says. The clean

20. Christians would see detachment as a corollary of another part of Jesus' teaching, wherein the believer is to "seek first the kingdom of God" (Matt 6:33), rather than seeking these other things. Detachment in this sense is again embodied and elicited in the story Christians are to follow.

21. Yun, *Buddhist Perspective on Compassion*, 11.

space, her friends, Noah Levine on the dais, all become living images for her. When asked about what specific images (of the Buddha, or Dharma teachers) located in the space do for her she responded, "they remind me of my role as a bodhisattva," the spiritual warrior, who gives herself for the "betterment of mankind."

Buddha image at Wat Thai Temple

In chanting one's life, the Buddhist awakens the Buddha nature and, in principle, the distinction between the inner and outer, the objective and subjective is dissolved. This integration is achieved throughout because the analytic weight is borne by the practice in its many forms. Of course there are metaphysical assumptions being made—about the self, the unitary nature of reality, and the common goal of all sentient beings. But these are not the focus of attention. Indeed, as Patrick of Against the Stream put it, the best Buddhist is constantly trying to become less Buddhist—that is less concerned about the ideas of Buddhism.

It has become clear that chanting, the complex image I am proposing, is in part an aesthetic practice. It implies integration, wholeness, and harmony, experiences that spark affection and motivate behavior. We remember that Patrick believes he can see the effects of such experience in the pictures of great Dharma teachers. The self-reference is gone from their faces, even their sense of place is deconstructed. When he looks at them, or at the Buddha, he sees compassion for himself and others. He finds these to be living images: "Wisdom and compassion embodied is a very beautiful thing that moves me to tears." But this is not about belief, he insists; it is "lived experience"—and that is the only way Buddhism can be validated.

Christians would certainly not ordinarily see their faith validated by "lived experience"; this would strike them as putting things the wrong way around. Rather the lived experience is itself validated by becoming rooted in the Christ story. The analytic weight is consistently borne by the narrative meaning. This seems natural to Christian believers. But the Buddhist way presses Christians to consider the tensions inherent in their imaginative structure: what social practices, if any, are *entailed* by this story? What ritual practice, or visual imagery and space, if any, best *embodies* this account?

Muslim Aesthetics of Worship: Spiritual Architecture

Muslim believers live out of a narrative, which, in some respects, resembles that of Christian believers. They believe God created the world and that he called Abraham to be the father of many nations. Though they trace their ancestry to Ishmael, Abraham's son by Hagar, they also honor Moses and Jesus as great prophets. But the final prophet was Muhammad, whom God sent to restore a pure form of monotheism. And they believe that finally, at the end of history, all people are morally accountable to God and will stand before him at the last judgment.

But the form this story line takes in Muslim prayers is much more concrete; it takes the shape of oral recitation and visual calligraphy—all embodied in the actual Arabic words of the Quran. Though these words surely recount events in the master narrative, the response of worshipers is not to the narrative but to the presence of God in the words—sung, written, and recited. And the response itself takes specific and concrete forms that include ablution, standing, bowing, and prostration.

So in the balance between meaning or narrative, image, and ritual practice, the focus of Muslim worship is much more concrete than either Christian or Buddhist practice. As in Buddhist meditation, the emphasis lies on the ritual practice, but, interestingly, for Muslims the role of artifacts (both visual and aural) is more prominent. I argued in an earlier chapter that the special role of the mosque—its layout, its design, even its orientation, the temporal structure provided by the daily prayers, along with the other required practices (significantly referred to as the five "pillars"), all suggest architecture as a useful trope for sketching in an Muslim aesthetics of worship.

As the structure and articulation of space facilitates and directs movement in architecture, so the structure of Muslim space and practice creates a special dynamic, a spiritual architecture. As Caroline Bynum points out, place is much more crucial to Islam than it is to Christianity.[22] But it is a place that is structured to facilitate specific practices even as it is directionally oriented toward Mecca. To elaborate this further, let me recall the claim of Saba Mahmood, that, in her study, the bodily practices furnish Muslim women places in which they forge their identity. These embodied practices, she argues, though enjoined, are not oppressive. Rather, Mahmood says, these women see such practices as "potentialities, the 'scaffolding' if you will, through which the self is realized."[23]

In what follows I want to develop the idea of Muslim worship as providing concrete spaces and physical occasions for the development of a self. Let me recall a few comments about what the act of prayer does for Muslim worshipers. Shafiq of the Iman Center feels closest to God during prayer. Prayer is not asking, he insists, "praying is when you humble yourself." Dr. Namazikhah, the founder of the Imam Center, conceives of prayer as a commitment to follow the righteous way. The recitation, even, or especially its aesthetic form encourages this. Shehla from the Mission Viejo Mosque feels the fine voice of one of the cantors "makes you concentrate in the prayer." You feel the verses more, she thinks, because Allah revealed them in rhythm. On the one hand respondents can insist that piety is not

---

22. Bynum, *Christian Materiality*, 275–77. Her conclusion that, for Muslims, relics are mostly "textual" fits well with our findings.

23. Mahmood, *Politics of Piety*, 148.

about something external, images or visual forms, but, as Shahed from the Islamic Center says, "it is more about something else that is taking place within." (Like many she prefers to close her eyes when she prays). Yet on the other hand, despite their protest against any dependence on images, many would agree with Mufti at the Islamic Center. He confessed that the more he studied Islam and focused on the Quran—reading it and memorizing it, the more a particular aesthetic preference emerged: "It was through looking at the script, the beauty of the stroke, and the way it looked on the page that—as opposed to an image of God, for example—it was through the beauty of the calligraphy that I found an expression of spirituality." These shapes, together with the beauty of the calls to prayer and recitation, provide a surface to his prayers that moves and directs him.

King Fahad Mosque

Surprisingly then, the Muslim response to God in worship depends more on visual and spatial cues, than either their Christian or Buddhist counterparts. Of course these artifacts and arrangements do not embody God in any literal sense, Muslims are emphatic on this point. Still the visual presence of the Quran and its calligraphy, like the oral presence in the call to prayer, are together expressive of the unique omnipresence of God. And so when the Muslim believers respond to this tactile presence, in the prostration and ablutions, they are very clearly embodying their theology. Their religion is performed in sensible forms that respond to these visual cues.

Earlier I noted Naim Shaw's insistence that a focus on concrete Arabic words of the Quran, of the names of Allah and Muhammad, and so on, imply an intellectual access to God, "something birthed through knowledge." But I argued there that this was more of an Old Testament expression of knowledge, rather than a modern, post-Enlightenment one. Knowledge involves a personal, even a spiritual union with the object. Here I would like to suggest that, just as the Muslim aesthetic may be correlated more to the Old Testament, its notion of the formation of the self is better understood in terms that are pre-modern (or better, non-modern) than modern. The "self" Muslims seek to form is not the Cartesian self of the West.

During the medieval period of Christianity, the mystics developed the ancient monastic tradition of prayer, over against the more popular memorial prayer, into a special vehicle of self-formation. In memorial prayer, adoration (and forms of supplication) were accomplished via reference to external forms and practices. (Recall Muir's comment that medieval believers were to adore and not to think.) But in mystical prayer the supplicant sought not so much to address prayers to God, as to make themselves into a medium of prayer. In other words, mystics sought to use prayer as a medium of self-formation.[24]

There are many differences between Christian mystics and Muslim prayer practices, but there is this striking similarity: Muslim prayer, while it may include elements of supplication, radically seeks to avoid memorial prayer. This is particularly characteristic of the mystical Sufi traditions of Islam where the prayer seeks union with God, but we found evidence of this among many of our respondents. These worshipers see prayer as a vehicle for the formation of the self, a site for enacting the connection between God and the worshiper. The Muslim seeks to make him or herself into the medium of prayer. As Abdul (from Ibad Allah) put it, you pray and then you "pick it up with you and put it on your back and move towards that goal." When you walk toward it, Abdul thinks, the creator will open the door for you.

---

24. For these ideas I am indebted to Niklaus Largier, "The Media of Prayer." This is consistent with Talal Asad's focus on the disciplinary matrix that medieval prayer involved. See the chapter, "Toward a Genealogy of the Concept of Ritual," 55–79, in *Genealogies of Religion*.

Thinking about Muslim prayer as a fundamental site for construction of the self helps us, I think, appreciate the unique relation between meaning, ritual, and image. We recall Saba Mahmood's argument that, for Muslim women, the practices themselves rather than the symbolic meaning, carry the analytic weight. Consider the case of Mona, who Mahmood describes. Mona tries to explain to another Muslim woman why it is critical to get up for morning prayer. This woman could not understand what morning prayer had to do with her everyday life. Mona responds:

> It means what your day-to-day deeds are . . . Does it hurt you when you see someone committing a sin or does it not affect you? These are the things that have an effect on your heart, and they hinder or impede your ability to get up and say the morning prayer . . . So when you do things in a day for God and avoid other things because of Him, it means you're thinking about Him, and therefore it becomes easy for you to strive for Him against yourself and your desires. If you correct these issues, you will be able to rise up for the morning prayer as well.[25]

Mahmood points out that this understanding of ritual contrasts with the widely accepted anthropological notion of ritual as separate and conventional. She argues: "One might say that for women like Mona, ritual performances are understood to be disciplinary practices through which pious dispositions are formed, rather than symbolic acts that have no relationship to pragmatic or utilitarian activity."[26] In our study, Nashmia the young woman born and raised in a cultured home in Afghanistan, supports Mahmood's point. She said, we recall, that during the ablution, while preparing for prayer, she felt closest to God. These practices shaped her as a Muslim. As she says: "[In] Western thought it is you that have control over your life and you make choices. But as a Muslim, I believe that there's a greater power and I have no choice . . . [or] very small choice. Like I believe always that God would be watching me and saying, 'that's not the choice you should be making.'"

So when you prepare for prayers "you always do your best and think that whatever you do is accepted by God." This is for her a disciplinary matrix, or in our terms, the architecture for the formation of a Muslim self.

25. Mahmood, *Politics of Piety*, 125.

26. Ibid., 128. She goes on to note that for these women when ritual is performed "for its own sake"—the usual understanding of ritual, without regard to how it contributes to the growth of piety, it is "lost power"—in our terms it becomes a "dead image."

Prostration at Masjid Ibad Allah

Christian ritual practices, by contrast, play a wholly different role. Rather than being a framework for the formation of the self, they are sites where "belief happens," to use David Morgan's term. The primary purpose of, say, the Eucharist, is to encourage deep personal and faithful belief. To be sure it has other secondary associations with moral practices, but it is chiefly about connecting one to the story of Christ, even, Christians believe, spiritually connecting one to Christ. Debbie, a reader at St. Monica's Catholic Church in Santa Monica, put her views of the Eucharist in terms that Protestants would also endorse: "Worship is the inner place . . . between the Eucharist and the Word, and then we come forward to worship; those two take hold and those two join hands." Here the practice of going forward to receive communion, enhanced no doubt by its visual and musical setting, becomes a living image. But, among these elements, it is the words that give life.

Nor does Buddhist meditation play the same self-defining role. Indeed the professed goal is to deconstruct the self, or, to put it in terms of bodhisattva practice, to dissolve the self into a compassionate life. Carl at Hsi Lai can appreciate the different bodhisattva images at the temple— one portraying wisdom, knowing how to help; another compassion, wanting to help. He bows to the images to "get myself in the mood." But his goal is to "do meditation better" . . . in order to "get control over what you respond to and how your respond." This response is typical, especially, of elite Buddhists we interviewed. It speaks of the tension between liberation from the cares of samsara and mindfulness and service within it. Though, sometimes, despite its claims, its strenuous pursuit of mindfulness carries a whiff of American individualism as well.

The Impact of the American (and Late Modern) Setting

This last comment raises a further question: What might this cultural context mean for the Muslim and Buddhist worshipers we interviewed? We touched on this in an earlier chapter, but here I want to return to the question and, in the process, nuance the claims of Saba Mahmood. Yasmin, the young woman who moved from India and prays at the Mission Viejo Mosque, works to become more God-conscious, though, she admitted, she still does "evil things." But she is sure America got her closer to God. When asked why this was so, she responded: "In India, it was more cultural than religious. My mother came with, you know, 'don't do this, this is not the culture' . . . [but] leaving my mom and coming here, and then the bad impression and everything over here, actually America helped me get more God-conscious." Nashmia, who grew up in Afghanistan, with religion but not in religion, as she put it, and prays at the Imam Center, explains her feeling about the difference. Here she is trying to live her life as much in submission to God as possible. She did not used to be like this, she admitted. But, she went on: "I think I became a better Muslim in America than I ever would have been in my own country, because there is no people of other faith[s there], and so you kind of take it for granted that everybody does the same thing and it becomes a daily routine. And here, when I came and I started going to school, people asked me a lot of questions . . . and I studied Christianity, and the more I studied Christianity, the more I became a better Muslim." In their countries religion was adopted unconsciously, along with the culture, but in America being religious necessarily involved a choice. And, as another young Muslim woman put it, when you have to choose, you have to think about it. You have to have reasons for the choice that you make. These responses resonated with things we heard from immigrant Buddhists. As we said earlier, one may not find it easier to be a Buddhist or Muslim in Los Angeles than in India, but it might be easier to be a *better* Buddhist or Muslim in L.A. Here then is a further variable

King Fahad Mosque

that may change the relative balance between practice and meaning that we have proposed. It may be true that, relatively speaking, the practice will still carry more analytic weight, as Mahmood argues for the women in Cairo, but the symbolic meaning will certainly be enhanced in the American setting. The choice makes this necessary.

Though there is resonance between American Muslim responses and the Buddhist adaptation to American culture, there are clear differences as well. Buddhist practices have proved remarkably adaptable throughout this faith's long history, as we have seen. So it is not surprising that Buddhism has found a home in America, even that it has adapted itself to the personal individualism of the religious culture of America. But when that same pluralist culture forces Muslims to choose their religious practice, it does not compel the same cultural adaptation as Buddhists. The architecture that shapes the Muslim self is a defined space which pointedly excludes much of the secular culture that lies outside its walls. The chanting of Buddhist practitioners, it seems, can more easily adapt to multiple settings than the spiritual architecture of Islam.

Reference to choice in religious preference raises again the specific context of these interviews—not simply geographically but chronologically as well. As Peter Berger has famously pointed out, the need to choose one's faith has come to characterize this period of Western religious history.[27] The pluralism of contemporary Western culture forces one to make choices about religion. But the findings of our study indicate that one does not simply choose a set of beliefs, rather one is attracted by and embraces a pattern of living images—even what is eventually a religious imagination. And becoming a member of one or another religious community is not simply a matter of changing beliefs. Carl, who was raised as a non-practicing Jew on Long Island, is a good illustration of this. He came across a book by the Dalai Lama and began to study Buddhist meditation, finding it compelling and motivating. Though he doesn't have a shrine at home, he appreciates the "regal quality" of the images and spatial arrangements at Hsi Lai Temple. He finds all of this authentic, not something "dreamed up recently." He mentioned appreciatively the fluid movement of the monastics—"they have their mind on the task . . . it feels good"—the precisely proportioned space of the temple, the process of meditation, and bowing to the Bodhisattva images. These together make up a way of life that attracted him. Though he claims "beauty doesn't move him," his own description of his journey to Hsi Lai betrays the significance of aesthetics for him. The pattern to which he is drawn includes assumptions about the way things are, to be sure. This could be articulated in some cognitive terms. But the *significance* of this is mediated and conditioned by concrete practices and visual arrangements; these feel good to him. In large part it is the aesthetics that draws him to Buddhism.

27. Berger, *The Heretical Imperative.*

Hsi Lai Temple

Being religious, whatever the cultural setting, involves adopting a particular configuration of practice and belief, with its unique balance between meaning and practice. Of course many who grow up in a tradition are not aware of making a conscious choice, but even these have a sense of being attracted to the spaces and practices of their faith. Consider how often respondents talk about their visits to their temple or mosque as lifting the pressures of life, of feeling at peace, relaxed, and safe.

As we saw in the introduction, attention to texts alone, however important, does not get at the way people actually inhabit their faith. We are now in a position to say more about this weakness. For one thing texts do not operate the same way in every tradition. Though the Quran plays a central role in Islam, this role is very different from the way the Bible functions for Christians, and further still from the Buddhist Scriptures for Buddhists. Moreover, texts and their meaning are put into play by the concrete performance of religion in space and over time. These performances moreover have a visual and aural shape, they comprise a pattern that attracts and nurtures believers. This is true, notwithstanding the protests of Muslims (and many Christians) that their praying has nothing to do with images or anything visual. In this sense our finding supports, and broadens, the claim of David Freedberg. He argued that the very idea of an aniconic faith is untenable. The will to make images, he thinks, cannot finally be suppressed.[28] Our study suggests his claim can be applied even more broadly. Attempts to banish aesthetics from religion, like those to banish images, are misguided and ultimately futile. The attraction of religion is invariably aesthetic as well as intellectual. People are attracted by the affective and aesthetic dimension of faith, whatever the conscious attention (or inattention) to aesthetics. Being a believer involves, in Rumi's wonderful image, "the taste of being at home."

There is a further danger associated with the focus on texts and creed that this study has suggested. A corollary of such a focus, in the context of interfaith conversation, is the inclination to subtly privilege the sharing of different beliefs over other types of exchange. On the basis of what we have discovered about religious imaginations and their complex interconnections between meaning, ritual, and image, the inadequacy of this approach is all too clear. A focus on belief is deficient for the simple reason that "belief" itself functions differently according to the relative weight given to the various elements of the religious imagination. Indeed, as we have seen, in the Buddhist tradition the notion of belief itself is problematic. In this sense, when it comes to interfaith dialogue, a focus on creeds and what we are calling linguistic representations may not only be inadequate, but it may constitute an unrecognized (if unintentional) imposition of the Christian—even the Protestant Christian imagination onto the conversation.

As I emphasized in the introduction, much is to be gained by comparative study of sacred texts and basic beliefs. This has been shown in the study of comparative theology and in the recent attempt to compare what is called "scriptural reasonings" of the major faith traditions.[29] As David Ford describes it, this initiative, by representatives of Christian, Jewish, and Muslim traditions, has sought to foster extended conversation about scriptural reading practices that is open to all people, religions, disciplines, and media.[30] From Ford's perspective this assumes, reasonably, that Christians have much to learn by reading the Bible in dialogue with those outside the

---

28. Freedberg, *The Power of Images*, 54–55.

29. See Ford, *Christian Wisdom*, chapter 8. The major literature of this movement are cited and discussed in this important chapter, which first appeared in *Modern Theology*.

30. Ibid., 273.

church[31] and that any attempt to deal with the core identity of any of these traditions "will inevitably involve its scripture."[32]

To be fair this young movement, involving some of the best thinkers of these traditions, readily acknowledges diverse practices and interpretations. And there is no attempt to provide authoritative overviews.[33] Ben Quash has noted the contested character of the very notion of "scripture" in these (and other non-Abrahamic) traditions, but argues that, "the category of 'scripture' meaningfully applies across traditions although accounts of what scripture is will vary greatly."[34] And David Ford allows that diversity in descriptions of interpretation lends these encounters "a 'dramatic' character, with many voices that cannot be integrated into a monologue."[35]

Nevertheless, though Ford describes movingly how hospitality turns into friendship within these small groups, and how these exercises become a "boundary crossing liturgy"—indeed probably the closest these different believers can come with integrity to "worshipping" together[36]—their setting in universities and academic meetings inevitably privileges what we are calling the linguistic representation of faith. While this movement has done much to create shared spaces that allow, as David Ford says, deeply held scriptural reasonings to have a constructive public face,[37] our research suggests such discussions could be enriched and extended by recognition of the role ritual practice, and visual and spatial cues, play in embodying and extending such reasoning. We have found that these other elements both facilitate and nuance the role that scriptures are allowed to play in these lived religions. In the conclusion I will consider the implications of this claim.

31. Ibid.

32. Ibid., 274.

33. Ibid., 276.

34. Quoted in Ford, *Christian Wisdom*, 274n2.

35. Ibid.

36. Ibid., 280–81.

37. Ibid., 281.

Meditating at Against the Stream

Conclusion: Aesthetic Trajectories and Religious Sharing

This study has intended primarily to compare the similarities and differences in Islam and Buddhism. But we have sought to situate this discussion in the larger context of interfaith sharing more generally, and in the conclusion I want to address this larger question. Earlier I proposed that members of different faiths, to more deeply understand each other, as well discussing differing beliefs or sacred texts, might gather around aesthetic artifacts. But now that I have described some of the specific "living images" of these traditions, the question arises: to what extent is such sharing possible? And what might be the potential—and limitations—of such exchange?

Obviously a weakness of this study was that respondents had no place or opportunity either to observe or respond to practices of another tradition. But what if this had been possible? What might such a shared space look like? Let me see if I can describe a place where members of different religious communities might gather around the symbolic practices and objects of faith traditions. Let's assume this space would not be defined by any particular imagination, but would represent a third, or shared space in which various religious imaginations may be displayed.[38] This may be

38. I have been helped in thinking this through by Locklin and Nicholson, "The

illustrated in the museum or gallery space or at a concert hall. To help us understand the difference between this and the previous (more specifically religious) space, let me make use of definitions Sister Wendy Beckett proposes in a recent study. She has distinguished between religious and spiritual art. The former represents the art resident in particular religious communities—calligraphy in Islam or icons in the Orthodox tradition. Beckett says of such art: "For the believer as such, the actual quality of the art is unimportant—the work stands or falls by its ability to raise the mind and heart towards the truths of faith."[39] And, we might add, such work does its best work in the context of the liturgical community and its practices. Spiritual art, she thinks, while it may grow out of particular religious communities, expresses religious truth in terms that may communicate to a broader public. Beckett describes the essence of spiritual art as taking us "into a realm that is potentially open to us, [where] we are made more what we are meant to be."[40] If something like this is possible, how might this idea be tested?

One possible testing ground, and a potential third (or shared) space, is provided by the Festival of World Sacred Music held annually in June in Fez, Morocco. Though promoted by an Islamic country, this festival provides a shared space for sacred musics from various parts of the world to be performed. During the festival held in June 6–12, 2008, my colleague Dr. Roberta King, a Christian scholar, conducted ethnographic interviews at the festival.[41] During a moving performance of American black gospel music on the first night, she reported: "I find myself suspended between two realms of my being. Is it true? Am I hearing Christian Gospel sung in a predominantly Muslim setting?"[42] Later in the week she sat in a concert by a Lebanese Muslim singing powerfully (in Arabic) about her love for her homeland. King could tell how deeply the audience felt the music and she found herself moved. When Muslims sitting near by asked if she had understood Arabic she had to admit that she did not; their disappointment was palpable. Much, she noted, could not be shared. On another night, the

---

Return of Comparative Theology," 479–514. There they make use of David Ford's image of a "tent" that is to be distinguished from the "campus" of the academy and the "house" of a particular worshiping community.

39. Beckett, *The Mystical Now*, 6.

40. Ibid., 7.

41. King, "Musical Gateways."

42. Ibid., 6.

platform was shared by the Munshidins (whirling dervishes) of a Damascus mosque and the Tropos Byzantine Choir of Athens; the combination of immobile singing and wild movement of the dervishes produced some awkwardness. Ethnomusicologist Laurent Aubier, whom King interviewed, expressed the ambiguity: He felt the attempt was worthwhile, but said: "I think that (musical) encounters are truly interesting in relation to the amount one sufficiently understands of the person's music with whom one is dialoguing. It was a bit as if they were people with different languages pretending to dialogue each one speaking their own (musical) language."[43] His comments are significant and support the findings of our study. The specific imaginations formed in communities of faith, what he calls (musical) languages, resist easy translation in public settings.

On another night two groups, an American gospel group and a Sufi ensemble from Pakistan, sought a kind of simultaneous experience—sharing the stage and calling on the audience to engage their musics together. It did not succeed, King thinks. The French newspaper *Le Figaro* on June 10, 2008 called this experiment a "cautious approach into one another's music." The article went on: "Too quickly there was too much respect that killed the respect; the hoped-for-fusion was not really achieved . . . Certainly improvisation created great risk. The immensity of the place and the fact that the 'spectacle' was suppose to be a new creation was intimidating. But the attempt, in the end, did not bear a great amount of fruit."[44]

Later in the week there was opportunity for the audience to share in a dance led by a women's ensemble from the Taureg tribe in Mali—here briefly the wall between performer and audience seemed to be breached. A Malawian man who did not know the Taureg dance joined in and enjoyed the experience. He reported: ". . . there was a generosity because I don't know the full extent of how they dance, I mean I kind of have an idea, and it is the generosity of spirit, of coming to dance with me, and no judgment, no lets do it like this. Just, again, an interplay! . . . following and leading."[45] Sharing is possible, there can be moments when the hoped for fusion is hinted at, and then it disappears. At such moments when the audience rises to dance or sing a common tune there can exist what Benedict Anderson called "imagined communities." In contrast to the dialogue and exchange that characterizes everyday life, Anderson notes, there can be moments when

43. Ibid., 8.
44. Quoted in ibid., 7.
45. Ibid., 11.

simultaneity becomes possible. "At precisely such moments, people wholly unknown to each other utter the same verses to the same melody. The image: Unisonance. Singing the Marseillaise, Waltzing Matilda, and Indonesia Raya provide occasions for unisonality, for echoes physical realization of the imagined community . . . How selfless this unisonance feels."[46] Some respondents reported to King that they were able to appreciate, sometimes deeply, music whose language they did not fully understand. One woman spoke of her experience in these terms: "I hope I can talk without breaking down because I've been so . . . my heart has been so open these last few days . . . For me the first afternoon performance—the Lebanese woman singing the early Christian songs was incredibly beautiful and moving."[47] Apparently the music was able to communicate to this woman at a deeply spiritual level, even though this was not her own tradition.

Here then is some evidence in support of Sister Wendy's claim that such music can involve deep spiritual sharing in which we are made "more what we are meant to be." The hospitality of this festival called to mind the warmth and welcome our researchers found in the temples and mosques where we did interviews and where we were also invited to meditate or pray. Surely there is much that members of different religious traditions share: common human experiences—life and death, shared histories, and a collective encounter with the physical world, and some form of transcendent reality. But our study has suggested that all of this takes peculiar forms in religious imaginaries, and it is construed by means of specific visual (or aural) epistemologies. If, as we have found, art and music, for adherents of religious faiths, finds its fullest expression in relation to these patterns, our encounter with aesthetic artifacts from other traditions has inherent limitations.

On the one hand, these forms are grounded in their own histories and religious cultures, and I as an outsider do not share this context; on the other hand, I am shaped by another set of factors, and so there is always the risk that I will interpret the art of another in terms of the visual habits and expectations I have learned from my tradition. Surely it is possible to enjoy and appreciate aesthetic forms of other traditions, especially when these are explained by friends from these communities. But we might put this in the form of a more modest claim: In hearing another's music, or seeing their art or ritual, we are offered glimpses into a community and an imagination that we cannot completely share, but that we are invited to taste. The implication

46. Anderson, *Imagined Communities*, 145.

47. King, "Musical Gateways," 10.

is that the door is opened by such experiences either to enter more fully, or return to the imagination of our home community.

Two recent experiences of artists in third spaces offer support for this more modest claim. Abdul Djalil Pirous is a highly respected Indonesian artist who was trained in Western secular styles in Bandung, Java. He achieved prominence in Indonesia and beyond for his work during the 1960s. In 1971 while visiting an exhibit of Islamic art at the Metropolitan Museum of Art in New York, he experienced his own taste of being at home. He realized, to his dismay, that the modern style he used was generic and said nothing about his own setting, or indeed his identity as Indonesian. The art he saw in New York was for him a call home; as a result he experienced a re-conversion to his Muslim heritage. He says of the experience: "I sacrificed myself, putting a limit on my free expression, but I came back to values that I could explore more frequently and more meaningfully in the Quran . . . I planted in the paintings concepts and philosophical values that would make them more enjoyable."[48] After he returned to Indonesia he rediscovered the motifs of his Muslim faith—some of which had been things his mother had embroidered when he was a child, and he began to incorporate them into his paintings.

A strikingly similar story is told by Yin Zhaoyang, a Chinese artist working in Beijing. During the 1990s Yin, while a student, also visited New York and was struck by the famous medieval Chinese Buddhist images in the Met. He too experienced a rediscovery of his own Chinese and Buddhist heritage, transforming these images onto canvases, coming to the conviction that the "beauty inherent in Buddhist art is beyond all beauty found in other art forms."[49] Though deeply moved by Buddhist imagery and the quest for inner tranquility, he has not himself become Buddhist. But this does not keep his work from reflecting a deeply Chinese and Buddhist sensibility. In one sculpture for example he depicts himself with legs crossed in meditation, with fists clenched at his sides, conveying his own personal struggle. He says: "the sculpture is a metaphor of our time; instead of striving towards a state of peace and balance, we often cannot help but feel anxious, agitated and helpless."[50]

48. George, *A. D. Pirous*, 60.
49. Rod-Ari, *Yin Zhaoyang*, 4.
50. Ibid., 4.

Pilar Langit ("Pillars of the Sky") A. D. Pirous (Indonesia), 1996.
125 x 145 cm, marble paste, gold leaf, acrylic on canvas. By permission
of the artist and Yayasan Serambi Pirous (Pirous Gallery Foundation)

Yin Zhaoyang, 2008, "Tearful Buddha," Chinese Marble, and red wine;
39 x 24 x 35 inches.

Third spaces then can provide safe places for outsiders (and former insiders!) to explore religious traditions. But do they provide places for people to experience a sense of the sacred that is unattached to any particular religious tradition? This would seem to be what Sister Wendy is calling for. And this is also the proposal of the late Alejandro García-Rivera who believes such places provide opportunity for an aesthetic experience of unity in diversity. He believes works of art provide an important dimension of the experience of what he calls interfaith. This can "engender and form in others the experiences of love that give hope in faith itself. In this way works of art provide an aesthetics that in helping to form faith also helps create an interfaith."[51] In one sense García-Rivera seeks a space where mutual spiritual encounters can take place, undoubtedly a worthy pursuit. He implies also that the beauty of a Bach cantata or a poem by Rumi transcends the particularity of their respective faiths, and speaks to the universal longing that constitutes human nature. This too is a helpful reminder. But at the same time he seems to reflect the common dismissal of ritual as something separate and conventional, that Mahmood critiqued above. He quotes approvingly J. Beichler and H. L. Bond's interpretation of Nicholas of Cusa: "When religious rite and form assume the place of religion, dissension and injustice abound: only the common experience of the reality of God, by whatever mode of experience is available to a given people comprises a genuine and reconciling spirituality."[52] This surely reflects the feeling of our Sufi respondents to our questions. But beyond these, our study has shown that religious traditions are invariably shaped by concrete patterns of practice that are seen as life-giving by believers. These patterns are nurtured by a history of lived experiences and associations. I would argue in fact that, with respect to the (non-Sufi) Islamic imagination at least, the role of practices are so central that such an attempt to transcend the particular forms is incoherent. Time and again we have seen ways in which specific practices are given meaning by the patterns they inhabit. Outside these settings, their impact is necessarily limited. Perhaps García-Rivera's (and Sister Wendy's) search for spiritual art, betrays an unconscious application of their own Catholic visual and sacramental hermeneutic. Clearly for the respondents in our study the experience of peace and, for the Muslim, the presence of God, is tied to specific practices and the patterns these have taken in their religious lives, and it would seem inaccessible without these. We did find

51. García-Rivera, "Interfaith Aesthetics," 190.
52. Ibid., 189

evidence of experience with the imagery or practices of other faiths, as when the images from a Christian past continue to impact those who have left this faith. But when some found meaning in an image or practice from another faith, this was invariably accomplished by re-siting these within their own, very different religious imagination.

This is not to say exposure to the music, art, and ritual of other faiths is ill-advised. On the contrary, it is only in the prolonged exposure to the living images of others, in one or another of these safe places, that we can know what can and cannot be shared and what light might be shed on the tensions resident in all our imaginations. In conclusion then, let me specify what positively such exchanges may facilitate.

To begin with, an encounter that starts with the recognition of difference allows us to get beyond the previous mistakes of comparative religionists who sought to find a universal religious essence at the heart of all religions. The recent interest in comparative theology recognizes that previous attempts to compare religions on the basis of a common definition of the "sacred" was at best a kind of pseudo-theology and at worst an unwitting perpetuation of the hegemony of Western modernity.[53]

At the same time it is sometimes possible for an outsider perspective to "see" something in the tradition that insiders cannot see but that one's different perspective illumines. This allows us both to learn something new and to return to our home traditions enriched by the experience of sharing. As the spiritual writer John Dunne puts this: "You find yourself able to pass over from the standpoint of your life to those of others, entering into a sympathetic understanding of them, finding resonances between their lives and your own, and coming back once again, enriched, to your own standpoint."[54]

---

53. Locklin and Nicholson, "Return of Comparative Theology," 486–87.

54. Quoted in ibid., 498.

Women at Masjid Abadallah

Finally, it is only by recognizing the depth and complexity of our own and others' religious imaginations that we can begin to work on the anxieties and prejudices that dog our attempts at mutual understanding. For a large part of the reason for the deep-seated suspicions that attend our encounters lies in the fact that imaginations can only be partly verbalized; so much rests in the level of assumptions and unconscious mental and visual habits.

The limits on sharing follow from the nature of imaginative constructions: they are dynamic fields that tend in one direction or another. And it is the "tending"—the dynamic—that matters. Titus Burckhardt has noted that each religious tradition has a particular economy. Because of this, he says, "it is out of the question that man [sic] should make use of all possible supports at the same time, or . . . follow two paths at the same time."[55] David Ford concurs: "No one can live and think bearing more than one of these core identities at the same time."[56] Islam and Buddhism are both religions of journey, but the roads and ends are different, and so is the look and feel of the path.

55. *SI II*, 164n1. He does go on to say this is true "despite the fact that the goal of all paths is fundamentally the same"—an assumption our study has inclined us to question.

56. Ford, *Christian Wisdom*, 294.

Visitors to other faiths, as John Dunne insists, will surely find they return home deeply enriched. But this also implies being a visitor is not the same thing as finding a home. For, as C. S. Lewis argued, the study of the basic structure of faith, or in our case an exposure to others' aesthetic objects, should never be seen as a substitute for adopting a particular faith. The study of "common" Buddhism and "common" Islam, like Lewis' notion of "mere" Christianity, is more like a hall out of which doors open into several rooms. The hall is a place to wait or try several doors, Lewis wrote, it is not a place to live in. For "it is in the rooms, not in the hall, that there are fires and chairs and meals."[57] Lewis ends with advice that we can endorse: "When you have reached your own room, be kind to those who have chosen different doors and to those who are still in the hall. . . . That is one of the rules common to the whole house."

---

57. Lewis, *Mere Christianity*, xi; the quote which follows is from p. xii. His argument was applied to Christianity in particular, I am extending it here to interfaith encounters.

Appendix

Art and the Visual in Communities at Prayer in Southern California

Participating Temples and Mosques

2008–2010

Buddhist Temples

Hsi Lai Temple, 3456 S. Glenmark Dr. Hacienda Heights, CA 91745.

Wat Thai Los Angeles, 8225 Coldwater Canyon Ave. North Hollywood, CA 91605.

Zenshuji Soto Mission, 123 S. Hewitt, Los Angeles, CA 90012.

Bodhi Path Buddhist Center, meets at Pasadena Senior Center, 85 E. Holly St, Pasadena, CA 91101.

Against the Stream Buddhist Meditation Society, 4300 Melrose Avenue, Los Angeles, CA 90029.

Islamic Mosques

King Fahad Mosque, 10980 Washington Blvd. Culver City, CA 90232.

Masjid Ibadillah, 2310 W Jefferson Blvd, Los Angeles, CA 90018.

IMAN (Iranian Muslim Association of North America) Cultural Center, 3376 Motor Ave, Los Angeles, CA 90034.

Orange County Islamic Foundation, 23581 Madero, Suite 101, Mission Viejo, CA 92691.

Islamic Center of Southern California, 434 S. Vermont Ave, Los Angeles, CA 90020.

Art and the Visual in Communities at Prayer in Southern California

Protocol for Buddhist interviews

November 2008

<u>Personal background</u>

1. Tell me about your family and religious background? Where were you born and raised? (When did you come to America?)

2. Were you exposed to the visual arts? To what extent?

3. Were you exposed to Buddhist imagery while growing up? During your education?
   For leaders:
   a. In your preparation (training) was there any teaching about imagery in relation to meditation?
   b. In your temple is there any instruction (by you or others) on imagery or visual elements that might assist meditation?

4. Growing up, what religious imagery was a part of your life? What religious practices? What memories do you have of these (either from your home or temple)? How has your religious faith been strengthened by these experiences?

5. In general what art do you love best? Describe your experience with this.

6. Where do you experience beauty most deeply?

7. What images or symbols do you connect with your present religious experience? Are these present in your home? How do these strengthen your Buddhist identity?

Worship in the Temple

8. How did you come to meditate in the temple you most identify with? (How often do you come?) What drew you there?

9. If you were to give a tour of this temple, what would you point out? What visual imagery is present?

10. What role do these images play in you meditation?

11. Are there special festivals when these visual elements or images become more important?

12. What do you like best about going to the temple?

13. What role does the space play in your temple meditation?

14. What elements in the temple encourage meditation? How do they do this?

15. How does the image of Buddha stimulate your meditation?

16. At what point in your praying do you experience meditation most deeply? What moves you in this way?

17. When you are in the temple what attracts your attention (draws your eyes) most? Does this contribute to meditation?

18. Are there any visual memories awakened by your visits to the temple?

Meditation in general (not necessarily connected to the temple)

19. How does your meditation affect your daily life?

20. Are there religious images in your home? How do these encourage meditation?

21. Have you ever had a specific experience with an image or sacred picture that has had an impact on your life? (Describe.)

22. Is there anything else about your religious life and faith that you would like to comment on?

Art and the Visual in Communities at Prayer in Southern California

Protocol for Muslim Interviews

November, 2008

Personal Background

1. Tell me about your family and religious background? Where were you born and raised? (When did you come to America?)

2. Growing up in this religious environment, what were you taught about art in relation to your faith?

3. Were you exposed to Islamic art while growing up? During your education? Afterward?

4. Growing up what religious imagery or practice was a part of your life? What memories do you have of these (either from your home or mosque)? How has your religious faith been strengthened by these experiences?

    For leaders add:
    a. Did your preparation (training) include any study of imagery in relation to prayers?
    d. Does the current teaching in the mosque (by you or others) include any references to imagery or visual elements?

5. In general what art do you love best? Describe your experience with this.

6. Where do you experience beauty most deeply?

7. What visual elements (images or symbols) do you connect with your present religious experience? Are these present in your home? How do these strengthen your Muslim identity?

Worship in the Mosque (Note: for women praying in the mosque is not required, so this part may be shortened.)

8. How did you come to pray in the mosque you identify with? (How regular is your attendance?) What drew you there?

9. Describe the space of the mosque. If you were to give a tour of this space what would be some visual aspects you would point out?

10. What role do these (the visual elements described) play in your prayers?

11. Are there any times of the year that symbols or visual elements are more prominent?

12. When you think of praying in the mosque what visual image (or images) comes into your mind?

13. What do you like best about going to the mosque?

14. What elements of the prayer time at the mosque encourage your sense of God's presence? What it is about them that does this?

15. Does the calligraphic imagery (of the Koran) contribute to your sense of "worship"? How?

16. When you are in the mosque what draws your eyes? Does this contribute to (or obstruct) your praying?

17. What visual memories are awakened during your time at the mosque?

Prayer in general

18. What role does the "place" where you pray, or the space of this place, play in your prayers? Are there any visual aspects important to your prayers?

19. At what point in your prayers are you most deeply moved or feel connected to God and others? What aspects do this for you?

20. What aspects of your prayers have the most impact of your daily life?

21. Have you ever had an experience with an image or picture that has had an impact on your spiritual life? (Describe.)

22. When have you experienced the Holy most deeply? At the mosque? In your daily prayers? The Hajj?

23. Is there anything else about your religious life and faith that you would like to comment on? About images and your faith?

Bibliography

Abdallah, John Ishvaradas. *A Sufi's Rumination on One World Under God.* San Pedro, CA: Star, 2002.

Abou El Fadl, Khaled. "Striking a Balance: Islamic Legal Discourse in Muslim Minorities." In *Muslims on the Americanization Path?*, edited by Y. Y. Haddad and John E. Esposito, 47–57. New York: Oxford University Press, 2000.

Albanese, Catherine. *America: Religions and Religion.* Belmont, CA: Wadsworth, 1981. 5th ed. 2012.

Anderson, Benedict. *Imagined Communities: Reflections on the Origin and Spread of Nationalism.* London: Verso, 1991.

Archer, Margaret S. *Being Human: The Problem of Agency.* Cambridge: Cambridge University Press, 2000.

Armstrong, Karen. *Muhammad: A Prophet for Our Time.* New York: HarperCollins, 2006.

Asad, Muhammad, trans. *The Message of the Quran: The Full Account of the Revealed Arabic Text Accompanied by Parallel Transliteration.* Bristol, UK: Book Foundation, 2003.

Asad, Talal. *Genealogies of Religion: Discipline and Reasons of Power in Christianity and Islam.* Baltimore: Johns Hopkins University Press, 1993.

Bass, Dorothy, and Miroslav Volf. *Practicing Theology Beliefs and Practices in Christian Life.* Grand Rapids: Eerdmans, 2002.

Beckett, Wendy. *The Mystical Now: Art and the Sacred.* New York: Universe, 1993.

Berger, Peter. *The Heretical Imperative: Contemporary Possibilities of Religious Affirmation.* Garden City, NY: Anchor, 1980.

Burckhardt, Titus. *Sacred Art in East and West.* Translated by Lord Northbourne. Louisville: Fons Vitae, 2001.

———. "The Spirituality of Islamic Art." In *Islamic Spirituality: Manifestation*, edited by Seyyed Hossein Nasr, 506–27. New York: Crossroads, 1991.

Bynum, Caroline. *Christian Materiality: An Essay on Religion in Late Medieval Europe.* New York: Zone, 2011.

Ch'En, Kenneth K. S. *Buddhism: The Light of Asia.* New York: Barrons, 1968.

Clooney, Francis X. "Comparative Theology." In *The Oxford Handbook of Systematic Theology*, edited by John Webster, Kathryn Tanner, and Ian Torrance, 177–205. Oxford: Oxford University Press, 2007.

Coomaraswamy, A. K. "The Origin of the Buddha Image." *Art Bulletin* 9/4 (June 1927) 287–328.

Dardess, George, and Peggy Rosenthal. *Reclaiming Beauty for the Good of the World: Muslim and Christian Creativity as Moral Power.* Louisville: Fons Vitae, 2010.

De Gruchy, John W. *Christianity, Art and Transformation: Theological Aesthetics in the Struggle for Justice*. Cambridge: Cambridge University Press, 2005.

Dreyfus, Herbert. *What Computers Still Can't Do*. Cambridge, MA: MIT Press, 1999.

Dunne, John S. *A Search for God in Time and Memory*. London: MacMillan, 1969.

Dykstra, Craig. *Growing the Life of Faith: Education and Christian Practice*. Louisville: Westminster John Knox, 2005.

Dyrness, William A. *How Does America Hear the Gospel?* Grand Rapids: Eerdmans, 1989.

———. *Poetic Theology: A Protestant Poetics of Everyday Life*. Grand Rapids: Eerdmans, 2011.

———. *Reformed Theology and Visual Culture: The Protestant Imagination from Calvin to Edwards*. Cambridge: Cambridge University Press, 2004.

———. *Senses of the Soul: Art and the Visual in Christian Worship*. Eugene, OR: Cascade, 2009.

Evdokimov, Paul. *The Art of the Icon: A Theology of Beauty*. Redondo Beach, CA: Oakwood Publications, 1990.

Ford, David F. *Christian Wisdom: Desiring God and Learning in Love*. Cambridge: Cambridge University Press, 2007.

Foulk, Griffith, and Robert Sharf. "On the Ritual Use of Chan Portraiture." *Cahiers d'Extreme-Asie* 7/7 (1993–94) 149–219.

Freedberg, David. *The Power of Images: The Study of the History and Theory of Response*. Chicago: University of Chicago Press, 1989.

García-Rivera, Alejandro. "Interfaith Aesthetics: Where Theology and Spirituality meet." In *Exploring Christian Spirituality: Essays in Honor of Sandra M. Schneiders*, edited by Bruce H. Lescher and Elizabeth Liebert, 178–95. New York: Paulist, 2006.

Geertz, Clifford. *The Interpretation of Cultures*. New York: Basic Books, 1973.

George, Kenneth M. *A. D. Pirous: Vision, Faith and a Journey in Indonesian Art, 1955–2002*. Bandung, Indonesia: Yayasan Serambi Pirous, 2002.

———. *Picturing Islam: Art and Ethics in a Muslim Lifeworld*. Chichester: Wiley-Blackwell, 2010.

Gibbs, Eddie, and Ryan Bolger. *The Emerging Church: Creating Christian Community in Postmodern Cultures*. Grand Rapids: Baker, 2005.

Goizueta, Roberto S. *Caminemos con Jesus: Toward a Theology of Accompaniment*. Maryknoll, NY: Orbis, 1995.

González-Andrieu, Cecilia. *Bridge to Wonder: Art as a Gospel of Beauty*. Waco, TX: Baylor University Press, 2012.

———. "Garcia Lorca as Theologian: The Method and Practice of Interlacing the Arts and Theology." PhD diss., Graduate Theological Union, 2007.

Harding, Susan Friend. *The Book of Jerry Falwell: Fundamentalist Language and Politics*, Princeton, NJ: Princeton University Press, 2000.

Heim, Mark. "Sharing Tensions in Buddhist and Christian Thought: An Experiment in Comparative Theology." Paper presented at the American Academy of Religion in Montreal, Quebec, November 7, 2009.

Isaac, Stephen, and William B. Michael. *Handbook in Research and Evaluation*. San Diego: Educational and Industrial Testing Services, 1997.

Johnson, Mark. *The Body in the Mind: The Bodily Basis of Meaning, Imagination, and Reason*. Chicago: University of Chicago Press, 1990.

Kamrane, Ramine. "Le Transcendent au service de l'immanent. L'art islamiste comme exemple d'art totalitaire en Iran." *Social Compass* 54/4 (Dec 2007) 603–11.

King, Roberta. "Musical Gateways to Peace and Reconciliation: The Dynamics of Imagined Communities at the Fes Festival of World Sacred Music." Unpublished paper, Fuller Theological Seminary, 2009.

Largier, Niklaus. "The Media of Prayer." At the conference "Cultures of Communication, Theologies of Media in Early Modern Europe and Beyond," UCLA, William Clark Library, Los Angeles, December 5, 2009.

Levitt, Peggy. *God Needs No Passport: Immigrants and the Changing American Religious Landscape.* New York: New Press, 2007.

Lewis, C. S. *Mere Christianity.* New York: Macmillan, 1952.

Lincoln, Bruce. *Holy Terrors: Thinking about Religion after September 11.* Chicago: University of Chicago Press, 2006.

Locklin, Reid B., and Hugh Nicholson. "The Return of Comparative Theology." *Journal of the American Academy of Religion* 78/2 (2010) 479–514.

Lopez, Donald S., Jr. *Critical Terms for the Study of Buddhism.* Chicago: University of Chicago Press, 2005.

Loverance, Rowena. *Christian Art.* Cambridge, MA: Harvard University Press, 2007.

Luhrmann, T. M. "Metakinesis: How God becomes Intimate in Contemporary US Christianity." *American Anthropologist* 106/3 (2004) 518–28.

———. *When God Talks Back: Understanding the American Evangelical Relationship with God.* New York: Vintage, 2012.

Luhrmann, T. M., Howard Nusbaum, and Ronald Thisted. "The Absorption Hypothesis: Learning to Hear God in Evangelical Christianity." *American Anthropologist* 112/1 (2010) 66–78.

Mahmood, Saba. *Politics of Piety: The Islamic Revival and the Feminist Subject.* Princeton, NJ: Princeton University Press, 2005.

Marsden, Peter V. "Religious Americans and the Arts in the 1990s." In *Crossroads: Art and Religion in American Life,* edited by Alberta Arthurs and Glenn Wallach, 71–102. New York: New Press, 2001.

Miller, Donald E., Jon Miller, and Grace Dyrness. "Religious Dimensions of the Immigrant Experience in Southern California." In *Southern California and the World,* edited by Eric J. Heikkila and Rafael Pizarro, 101–32. Westport, CT: Praeger, 2002.

Morgan, David. *The Sacred Gaze: Religious Visual Culture in Theory and Practice.* Berkeley: University of California Press, 2005.

Muir, Edward. *Ritual in Early Modern Europe.* 2nd ed. Cambridge: Cambridge University Press, 2005.

Nabhan-Warren, Kristy. "Embodied Research and Writing: A Case for Phenomenologically Oriented Religious Studies Ethnographies." *Journal of the American Academy of Religion* 79/2 (2011) 378–407.

Nasr, Seyyed Hossein, ed. *Islamic Spirituality I: Foundations.* World Spirituality 19. New York: Crossroad, 1987.

———, ed. *Islamic Spirituality II: Manifestations.* World Spirituality 20. New York: Crossroads, 1991.

Nattier, Jan. "Visible and Invisible: The Politics of Representation in Buddhist America." *Tricycle* 5/1 (1995) 42–49.

Ortner, Sherry. *Anthropology and Social Theory: Culture, Power and the Acting Subject.* Durham, NC: Duke University Press, 2006.

Pal, Pratapaditya, ed. *Buddhist Art: Form and Meaning.* Mumbai: Marg, 2007.

Partridge, Michael. "Performing Faiths—Patterns, Pluralities and Problems in the Lives of Religious Traditions." In *Faithful Performances: Enacting Christian Tradition*, edited by Trevor Hart and Steven Guthrie, 75–90. Aldershot, UK: Ashgate, 2007.

Promey, Sally, and Shira Brisman. "Sensory Cultures: Material and Visual Religion." In *Blackwell Companion to Religion in America*, edited by Phillip Goff, 177–205. Malden, MA: Blackwell, 2010.

Rod-Ari, Melody. *Yin Zhaoyang: Radiation*. Los Angeles: DF2 Gallery, 2008.

Rumi (Maulana Jalāl al-Dīn Rūmī). *The Glance: Songs of Soul-Meeting*. Translated by Coleman Barks. New York: Viking, 1999.

Stambach, Amy. *Faith in Schools: Religion, Education and American Evangelicals in East Africa*. Stanford, CA: Stanford University Press, 2010.

Taves, Ann. "Religion in the Humanities and Humanities in the University." *Journal of the American Academy of Religion* 79/2 (2011) 289–310.

———. *Religious Experience Reconsidered: A Building Block Approach to the Study of Religion and Other Special Things*. Princeton, NJ: Princeton University Press, 2009.

Taylor, Charles. *Modern Social Imaginaries*. Durham, NC: Duke University Press, 2004.

Yoshinori, Takeuchi, ed. *Buddhist Spirituality I: Indian, Southeast Asian, Tibetan and Early Chinese*. New York: Crossroads, 1995.

———. *Buddhist Spirituality II: Later China, Korea, Japan and the Modern World*. New York: Crossroads, 1999.

Yun, Hsing. *Buddhist Perspective on Compassion*. Fo Guang, Shan, Taiwan: Buddha's Light International Association, 2001.

Zachman, Randall C. *Image and Word in the Theology of John Calvin*. Notre Dame, IN: Notre Dame University Press, 2007.

Zago, Marcello. "The New Millennium and Emerging Religious Encounters." *Missiology* 28/1 (2000) 5–18.

7364582R00095

Made in the USA
San Bernardino, CA
04 January 2014